WORLD WAR 1 HISTORY FOR KIDS:

Stories of Courage, Cautionary Tales & Fascinating Facts to Inspire & Educate Children about The History of WW1

HISTORY BROUGHT ALIVE

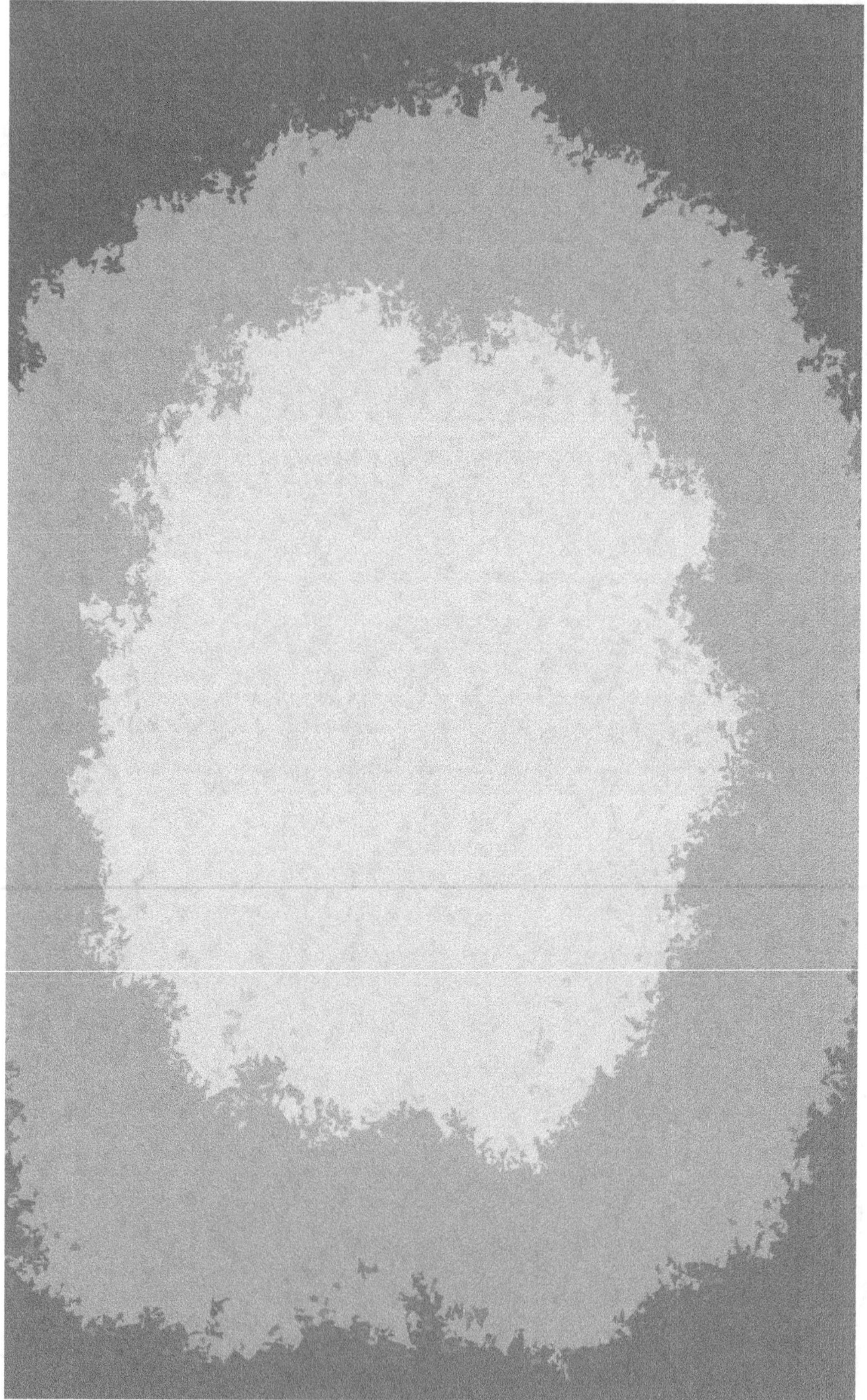

WORLD WAR 1
HISTORY FOR KIDS

Published 2023 by History Brought Alive

FREE BONUS FROM HBA: EBOOK BUNDLE

Greetings!

First of all, thank you for reading our books. As fellow passionate readers of History and Mythology, we aim to create the very best books for our readers.

Now, we invite you to join our VIP list. As a welcome gift, we offer the History & Mythology Ebook Bundle below for free. Plus you can be the first to receive new books and exclusives! Remember it's 100% free to join.

Simply scan the QR code to join.

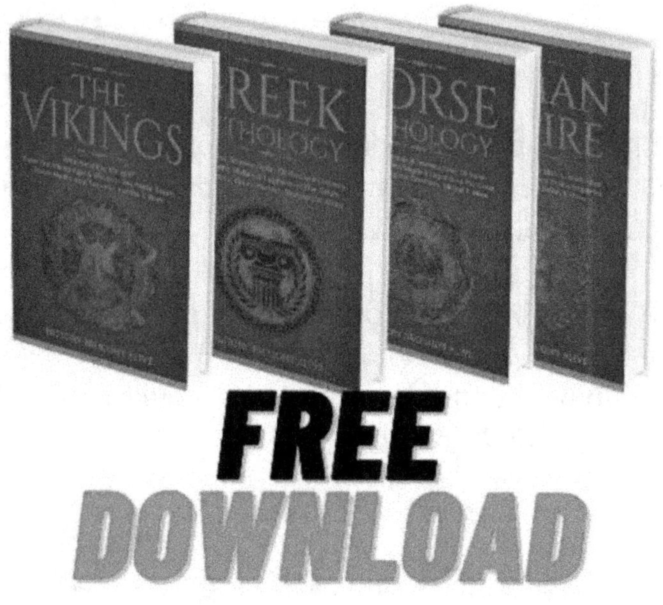

<u>Keep up to date with us on:</u>

YouTube: History Brought Alive

Facebook: History Brought Alive

www.historybroughtalive.com

CONTENTS

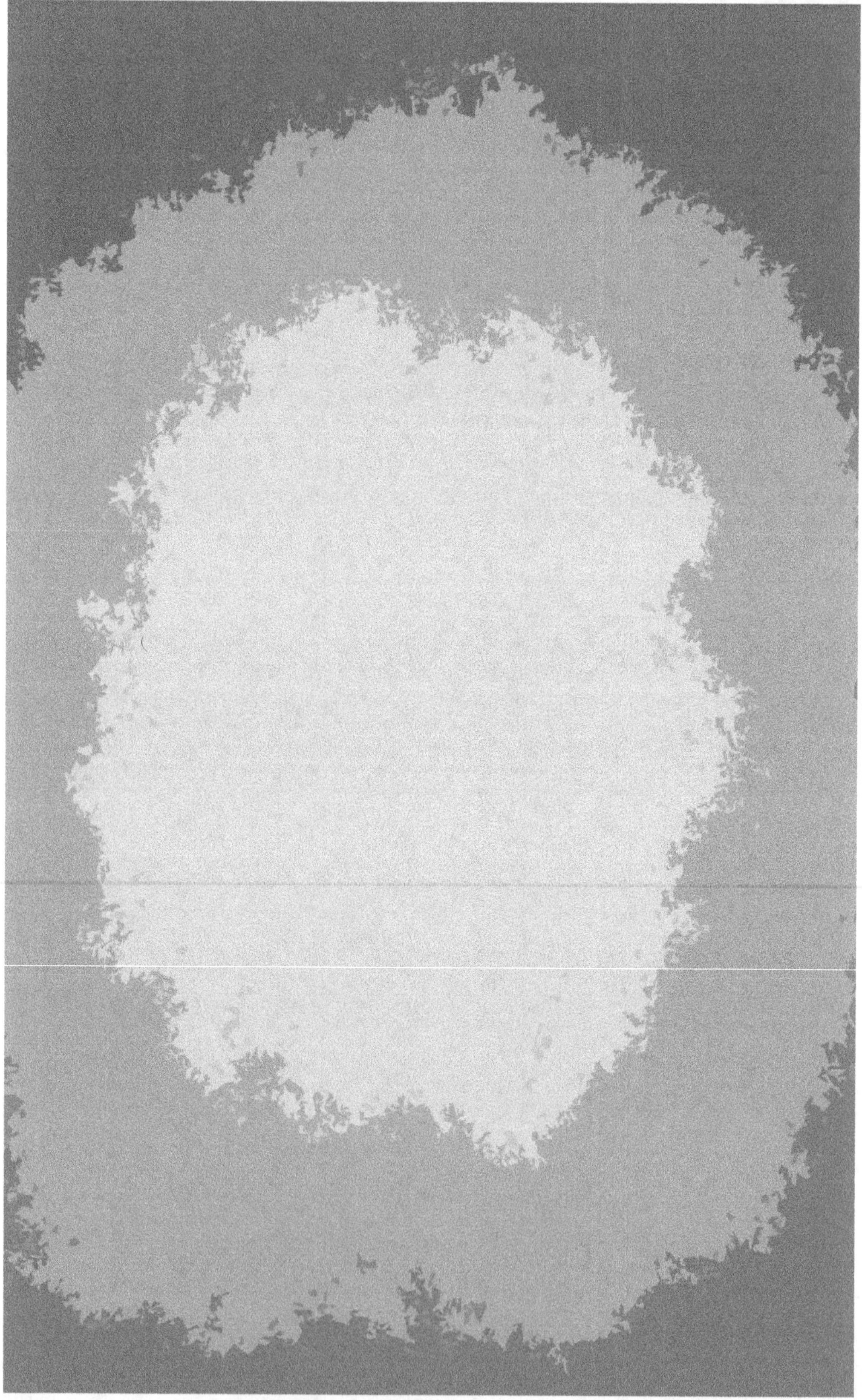

INTRODUCTION

More than a century has passed since the beginning of World War 1. That might seem like a lifetime ago, but guess what? We have a time machine of our own that can return us to this amazing place! Reading about this incredible period in history is like taking a trip back in time. So prepare to board our make-believe time machine by selecting your time travel outfits. Our travels are about to take us to a period in history when things were quite different from the way they are now.

Now you might think that history is boring. Well that's wrong! History is a treasure trove filled with exciting stories waiting to be uncovered. These stories are like magic carpet rides that can take us away to distant lands and long ago eras. Close your eyes and imagine yourself sitting next to a fireplace wrapped in a cosy blanket with a wise storyteller speaking tales of bravery, friendship and challenges faced by people in the past. Suddenly you find yourself right there in the heart of the story experiencing every moment.

Perhaps you're wondering why you should study World

War I? Well try to think of it this way. Imagine our history as a puzzle in which many pieces are missing. World War 1 is an important piece that influenced how the world is today. Life, culture and nations were at an important turning point back then. We can fill in the blanks from the past by going back in time to explore those days. In the end, this will help us to understand why the world was this way and how it became to be today.

Have you ever looked at one of your old family photo albums? The kind where you see pictures of your great great grandparents when they were kids just like you. Or ones from when your parents were younger, or even when you were just a baby. These photos help us understand where we came from and how our family has changed over the years. Studying history is a lot like looking at pictures in a huge photo album. Learning how things work, why they are the way they are, and how the world, which is like our extended family, has evolved over time. But why World War I specifically? Well this is the first chapter in a thrilling book series! Our other book explores the history of World War 2.

World War 2 History For Kids: A Timeline of Fascinating Facts, Characters and Stories of Courage that Inspire & Educate

https://www.amazon.com/dp/B0C7QW6T66

You see, stories have the incredible power to take us back into time. Through them we can step into the shoes of those people who lived there, long ago such as the heroes of World War 1. Seeing the world through their eyes, experiencing their hopes, fears and dreams allows us to learn from their experiences. Stories are great for teaching as well as entertainment. They show us how to be strong in the face of adversity, accepting toward others, and resilient after setbacks. There are countless incredible tales in history, all of which offer invaluable life lessons.

Along this journey you'll learn about the incredible individuals who fought on the front lines and back home during World War 1. As you travel back through time, you'll hear their accounts, learn about their lives and experience what they went through. Besides learning there is another great benefit. Through learning about their experiences it will help make you a stronger, more confident person.

Are you ready to learn? Well we sure are because our time machine is all set and the adventure is about to begin! Buckle up, time travellers, because you are about to experience the past as it was during World War 1. Get ready to enter our time machine and travel back to one of the most important events of the 20th century. It's also a major turning point in human history!

Here's a sneak peek at some of the content you'll find in the book.

In part one we venture out on the "THE ROAD TO WAR"

CHAPTER 1: THE CAUSES OF WORLD WAR

Discover the amazing story of how, and why World War 1 began. Explore the arms race, Balkan conflicts and a shocking assassination that sparked the flames of war.

CHAPTER 2: THE START OF WORLD WAR

Dive into the dramatic start of World War 1 as nations clashed and global alliances were tested. Witness the early battles that set the stage for the long struggle ahead.

CHAPTER 3: LIFE IN THE TRENCHES

Descend into the grim and muddy world of trench warfare.

Learn about the daily life, challenges and strategies of soldiers who fought in the trenches as the war raged on.

CHAPTER 4: HOME FRONT HEROES

Discover the heroes on the home front, who played an important role in supporting the war. From women's contributions to kids just like you.

In part two we witness the "MAJOR BATTLES"

CHAPTER 5 WESTERN FRONT 1914 TO 1916

Witness the early days of World War 1, where war was spreading like wildfire across the battlefields of Europe.

CHAPTER 6: FIGHTING FOR CONTROL OF THE SEAS

Set sail and witness battles on the oceans as ships, submarines and strategies crashed on the high seas.

CHAPTER 7: FRESH CHALLENGES & SOUTHERN THEATRES

Journey to the southern parts of Europe where the war was fast progressing like a fierce storm. Unravel this complex era as allies and enemies shifted.

CHAPTER 8: THE OTTOMAN EMPIRE

Venture into the vast Ottoman Empire to learn about their involvement in the war, including the Gallipoli Campaign, the Armenian Genocide and the Arab Revolt.

CHAPTER 9: ADVENTURES IN THE EAST: HEROES, CHANGES, AND BIG BATTLES

Explore adventures on the Eastern Front as new nations including Romania and Russia joined the war. Experience the massive impact of the Russian Revolution and how it led to Russia's withdrawal from the war.

In part three we enter the "FINAL YEARS"

CHAPTER 10: AMERICA JOINS THE FIGHT

Learn how the United States, a sleeping giant, finally entered the war and shifted the balance of power to the Allies.

CHAPTER 11: HIGH-STAKES ON THE WESTERN FRONT

Explore the high-stakes gamble of the Nivelle Offensive and its consequences on the Western Front.

CHAPTER 12: THE SINAI AND PALESTINE ADVENTURE

Embark on an adventure in the desert as the Allied forces pushed into the Middle East, capturing key territories.

CHAPTER 13: THE ALLIES MAKE THEIR FINAL PUSH FOR VICTORY

Witness the German Spring Offensive, its initial successes and later challenges that changed the course of the war. Experience the Hundred Days Offensive, a remarkable period when the Allies launched a series of successful offensives that led to the war's end.

CHAPTER 14: PEACE AT LAST

Discover the armistice agreements, the Paris Peace Conference and the signing of the Treaty of Versailles that marked the end of the war.

CHAPTER 15: A FRAGILE PEACE

Learn how nations worked together to rebuild after the

devastation of the war and faced the challenges of reconstruction in a fragile peace.

CONCLUSION

Reflect on the profound impact of World War 1, the lessons learned and the lasting legacy it left on the world stage.

APPENDICE ONE

Discover "the time traveller tool kit" which includes many exclusive bonuses, extra content and much more for the most diligent young historians.

APPENDICE TWO

Discover the technology advancements in World War 1. Including weapons, medical inventions and innovations plus the impact of technology on World War 1.

PART ONE:
THE ROAD TO WAR

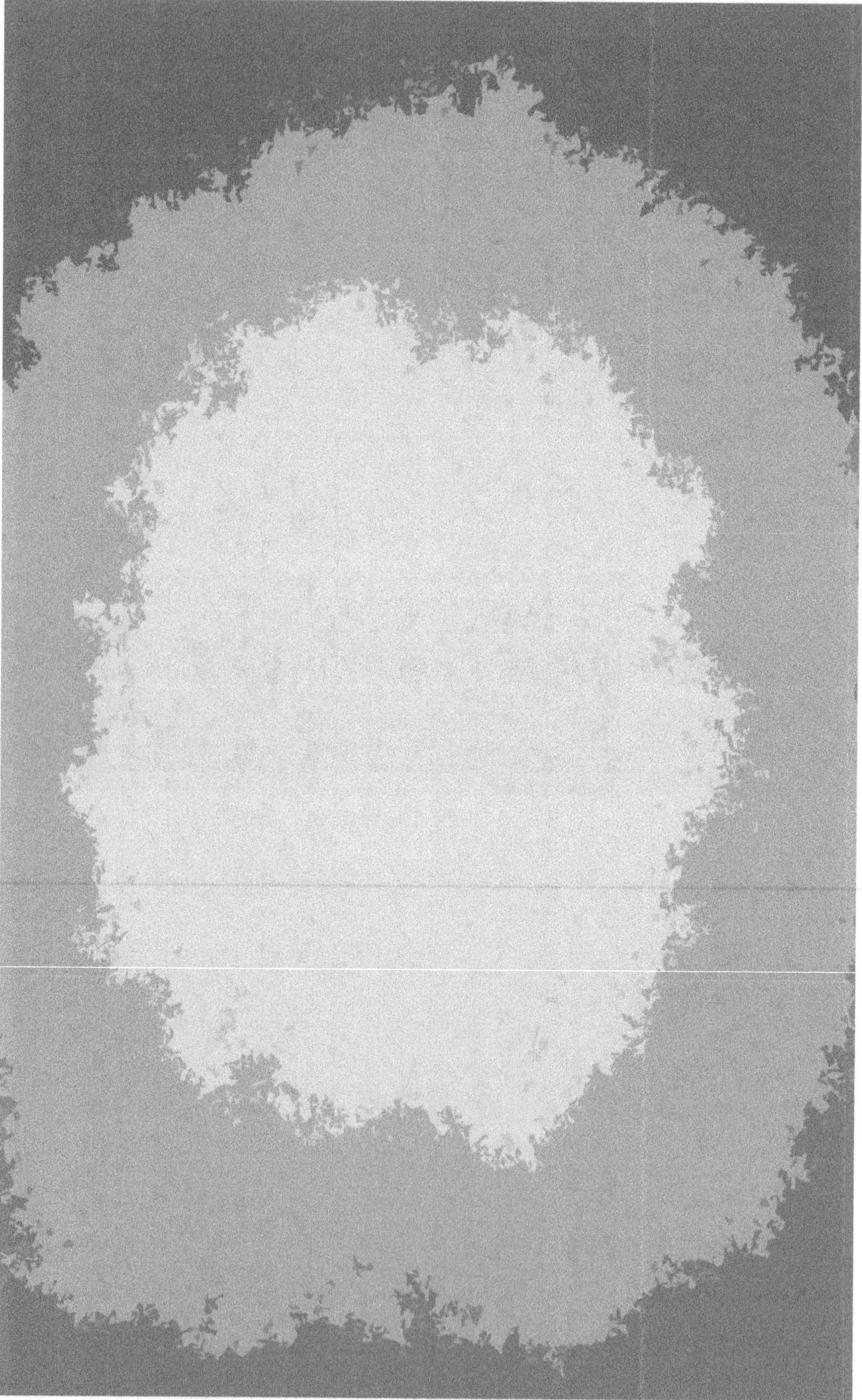

CHAPTER 1
THE CAUSES OF WORLD WAR I

Hello, and welcome to the beginning of our study into the early history and causes of World War 1. Join us as we visit the past to see how life was over one hundred years ago. In those days, the world was like a jigsaw puzzle with many pieces, each having its own unique arrangement. The world was changing and with it came increased tension. It was like the inside of a hot oven where the tension and temperature was steadily rising. Many factors and narratives were causing this build up. Now as we delve into the background of this global conflict, we'll find out what those were and how they played a role in the war.

Arms race

In the late 19th to early 20th century, nations in Europe had built up enormous armies with powerful defences. It was like a contest to see who could become the strongest. Battleships with massive cannons, lethal weapons, and strong soldiers appeared to be multiplying daily in the struggle to come out on top. But as each nation built a stronger military the more nervous their neighbours became.

Imagine if you lived in a neighbourhood and all the houses around you kept building higher walls. You might start to wonder why they are doing that? Are they hiding something or are they preparing for something? Well this is exactly how it felt for the nation's competing against each other. Suspicion spread like a fog as nations competed to build the mightiest militaries. It was like a monstrous storm was building, complete with dark, threatening clouds just waiting for thunder to clap.

Conflicts in the Balkans

Now let's hop on our time machine and head over to the Balkans region. This area of Europe was missing a lot of information, despite the fact that it was an important piece of the overall puzzle. Serbs, Croats, Bosnians and many others have all called this extraordinary place home at one time or another. But just like a puzzle where pieces don't often fit together these groups of people didn't always get along so well. Rivalries quickly formed as the tensions between the groups grew like a raging river.

Imagine the region like a large apartment building where they all lived, but where each person wished to decorate their hallway in their own way. Conflict was common as various groups pursued their own goals and old wounds reopened. As time passed the heat was slowly building up to a new level. All it needed was a small spark to ignite it into a huge fire. That spark was about to come in an event that would shake the whole world.

Sarajevo Assassination

Deep in the heart of the Balkans nestled like a jewel in a crown was a lively city named Sarajevo. It was very much like a busy marketplace, full of people from all walks of life going about their daily lives. On one fateful day, June 28th, 1914 this ordinary city would become the stage for an extraordinary event that would send shockwaves across the globe.

At the centre of this event was the assassination of Archduke Franz Ferdinand, of Austria-Hungary and his wife Sophie, The Duchess of Hohenberg. The Archduke was no ordinary person. He was next in line to be the King of the Austrian-Hungarian Empire. Sophie, his wife, was dearly in his heart and their love story was one that went against the strict rules of royalty. The couple took a visit to Sarajevo, but it was not a normal royal visit. On the anniversary of a significant battle, they came to pay their respects and show appreciation to the locals. They looked at it as a chance to make a fresh start and spread goodwill across their empire.

Things were far from calm in the Balkans. The shifting of these nations around like a jigsaw puzzle had caused increased tensions in the area. Bosnia and Herzegovina had been annexed by Austria-Hungary in 1908 and this had caused significant tension. Wait a minute, what does annex mean? Annex - means that a country takes over a new piece of land and makes it a part of their own country. It's kind of like when you add a new piece to your jigsaw puzzle and it becomes part of the bigger picture. But here's the important thing. When a country annexes another piece of land, it usually has to follow some rules and talk to other countries to make sure everyone is okay with it. Just like you might ask your friends if it's okay to add your piece to their puzzle. Annexing is like adding a new piece to a country's puzzle, but it's done in a way that makes sure everyone agrees and it's fair for everyone involved.

Now back to the story! Amongst the building tension a

secret organisation known as the Black Hand was formed. Gavrilo Princip was a famous member of it. During the busy day of June 28th, 1914 in Sarajevo, Princip and his group spotted a chance to further their cause. Many in the region saw the royal Archduke's visit as a symbol of their oppression and they wanted to be freed from it. With a heart full of determination and a pistol in his hand, Princip stepped forward. He took aim and shot at the Archduke, who stood for an entire system. The Archduke was killed when he collapsed. (King & Woolmans, 2013) (Butcher, 2014)

The assassination was not just an act of violence but it became a spark that ignited the flames of World War I. Austria-Hungary was furious over the assassination and held Serbia responsible. They declared war on Serbia which set off a chain reaction of events leading to a global conflict. Sareajo which was once a city famous for its culture and diversity had now become the centre of a world changing event. From this point onwards the world was plunged into the darkness of war and all because of those fateful shots fired on that day.

The assassination's effects echoed globally, much like the sound of gunfire did through Sarajevo's streets. Serbia was held responsible by Austria and Hungary. But Serbia had many allies just like friends in the neighbourhood who came to their rescue. Russia, which was a powerful nation at the time, felt its duty to protect Serbia. Russia too had its own set of allies including France and the United Kingdom. It was like each country was tangled in a spider web of alliances and the threads were slowly being pulled apart.

Imagine a line of dominoes; if one falls, the others will fall. The first domino falling was the assassination of the Archduke. Dominoes then started to fall one by one. Russia sent military aid to Serbia. War was declared by Germany against Russia. The United Kingdom and France joined in to keep their word and back Russia. The dominoes began to fall and soon enough World War 1 had begun. Europe quickly became like a huge thunderstorm. Suddenly, armies from different countries began to face off and fight each other. One must keep in mind that this was no ordinary conflict. It was a war on a scale unlike anything the world had ever seen before. Later we will look at this in much, much more detail so stay tuned! This was the start of World War 1, which would alter the course of history in ways no one could have predicted. The term "July crisis" was coined to describe the dramatic increase in tension that occurred that month of 1914.

That very first domino falling which was the assassination in Sarajevo amongst the rising tension had begun the chain reaction of events plunging the world into the depths of conflict. It was a cautionary reminder of how seemingly small events can have far reaching and devastating consequences. We must learn that when we do bad things the consequences can be much greater than that act itself. Because of these events, the world was about to plunge into the darkness and chaos of World War 1. A war like never before.

*Archduke Franz Ferdinand,
of Austria-Hungary and his wife*

CHAPTER 2
THE START OF WORLD WAR 1

Greetings, returning young readers! The dramatic events that led up to World War 1 are now well known to you. In the last chapter we saw how early moves and alliances played out. Now we're about to explore what happened next. In this chapter, we're going to dig even deeper into the unfolding drama of the war. Prepare yourselves for another exciting exploration where we'll journey deeper into the heart of World War 1 history.

When the war began it was like a massive curtain rising on a grand play with many countries stepping out onto the world stage. Now let us introduce some of those key players. Without getting into all the confusing battles (we'll do that later), let's explore why Austria-Hungary, the Ottoman Empire, and Germany allied together. Furthermore we will explain why France, Russia, and the United Kingdom allied themselves against them.

At the start of the 20th century, huge countries like Austria-Hungary, Germany and the Ottoman Empire all wanted more land and power. Imagine if you really liked cars and you wanted to have lots and lots of them. Even if you already had quite a few! Well those countries began annexing territory from others without asking. Similar to taking cars from one another. Some of these countries were friends with each other and when one of them got into a fight with another country, their friends wanted to help them out. It's a bit like if one of your friends had a problem with someone. You would stand by your friend's side to support them. Austria-Hungary, Germany and the Ottoman Empire had similar goals and joined together to become known as "The Central Powers". But all this collecting of land and helping friends led to serious problems. Eventually as we learned earlier this tension combined with events such as the assisination exploded into a huge, sad event known as World War 1.

Now on the other side of The Central Powers, there were three good friends. France, Russia and the United Kingdom. They didn't like how those greedy countries were taking things from others because they believed in something called democracy. This means that people should have a say in how their countries are run and that everyone should be treated fairly. Together they decided to stand up to the greedy countries, who were like bullies in a way. Ultimately they wanted to stop them from taking more land and causing trouble. Thus they joined forces and became known as the Allies. The Central Powers were the "enemy" that France, Russia, and the United Kingdom decided to unite against in World War 1. Germany, Austria-Hungary, the Ottoman Empire and Bulgaria were all members of this group of Central Powers.

Asia and the Pacific Theatre in World War I

Beyond Europe, the impact of World War 1 was felt around the world. The waves of war could be felt all the way across Asia and to the Pacific. The German Empire controlled many Pacific colonies, including Papua New Guinea and Samoa. However, the Allied forces could count on their friends in Australia and New Zealand for support there. By taking control of these nearby regions, they hoped to increase their influence. The Pacific region erupted in violence. Australia invaded Papua Guinea, and New Zealand occupied Nazi-occupied Samoa.

Japan, another Asian country, also decided to join the global conflict. In the beginning, they attacked Germany. Japan saw the war as an opportunity to seize German-controlled territories in the Pacific. In particular, Japan aimed to gain control of German-controlled territories in China's Shandong Peninsula and the Pacific islands of Micronesia. They set their sights on annexing various islands and territories in the Pacific. They also planned to seize control of what the Chinese call "Treaty ports." But there was a ship from Austria-Hungary called SMS Kaiserin Elisabeth in one of those places, called Tsingtao. Japan asked nicely for the ship to leave, but Austria-Hungary said no. Japan got angry and declared war on Austria-Hungary too. They even attacked the ship with their aircraft. (Fenby, 2014)

In just a few months, Japan and its friends in the Allies managed to take control of all the places that belonged to Germany in the Pacific. They left only a few ships that were causing trouble and some people who didn't want to give up in New Guinea. It was like a big game of capture the flag, but with countries and territories instead!

The African Theatre of World War I

Many African countries were also involved in World War 1. Imagine the world as a giant chessboard with different nations moving their pieces. Africa played an important role on this chessboard. Germany had colonies in Africa and the Allies wanted to capture them. The first battles took place in East Africa where German General Paul von Lettow-Vorbeck led a daring campaign. It was kind of like a high-stakes game of hide and seek with the German general using cunning tactics to outsmart his opponents. (Gaudi, 2017)

Indian Support for the Allies

As a developing nation, India had a major impact on World War 1. At the time, India was a colony of the United Kingdom. Essentially this meant they were under the United Kingdom's rule. Back then it was a huge empire. Indian troops fought on both the European and the Middle Eastern fronts. Valiantly they fought on the side of the Allies and made important contributions to their cause as they smashed across battlefields like a mythological elephant.

The contributions of Indian troops in World War 1 not only demonstrated their role as valiant warriors but also paved the way for later political changes in India. The recognition of their sacrifices played a part in their struggle for independence. To this day the legacy of brave Indian soldiers continues to be remembered and honoured.

World War 1 was fastly progressing and the world watched on as nations class clashed on multiple fronts. But dear time travellers as we journey through this epic tale we're about to face some harsh realities. As the war evolved it would soon plunge into a new challenging chapter. A chapter filled with mud, trenches and tough times. Brace yourselves as our next adventure will take us deep into the trenches where we'll discover the harsh and relentless nature of trench warfare.

Indian Soldiers during World War 1

CHAPTER 3
LIFE IN THE TRENCHES

Welcome back once again fearless time travellers! In the last chapter we saw how the war was advancing as the world was captivated with clashes on multiple fronts. In this new chapter it's time to face a harsh reality. As the war was evolving it was thrust into a new era lined with trenches and extremely tough times. In this chapter we're going to enter into the trenches where you'll discover the gritty and harsh nature of trench warfare. So prepare yourselves for a difficult journey that lies ahead.

Imagine your favourite pair of shoes. The ones you like to wear for adventures with friends or for when you play sports. Now imagine those shoes were covered in thick, gooey mud that sticks with every step. That was only a small sample of what it was actually like for soldiers on the front lines. Throughout the battlefields, trenches dug into the mud acted as the "arteries." But these tunnel networks were much more than just trenches; they were an underground world where soldiers lived and died. Brave soldiers would spend weeks and often months in those confined spaces where they were faced with isolation, boredom and the fear of sudden death. Their stories are a testament to the spirit and strength of humans.

Trench life was a daily struggle for survival. Not only did soldiers face the threat of enemy attacks but they were also exposed to extreme elements, diseases and the constant psychological strain of combat. The muddy, cold and wet conditions would often become flooded and infested with rats. When it rained, it was even more difficult to move around. Imagine trying to cross a never-ending puddle and there's no way of escaping it. For days on end the rain would pour down relentlessly turning the trenches into rivers of mud. Soldiers couldn't just go indoors to dry off or warm up. There was nowhere to stay but the trenches, so they had to endure those cold wet conditions with mud squelching beneath their feet.

There was no gourmet cooking going on in the trenches either. Biscuits, canned meat and watery soups were on the daily menu. The canned meat was tough and gritty and the biscuits were like rock hard crackers. Such meals were a far cry from the tasty meals that we now enjoy at home with our families. But despite the lack of tasty food the brave soldiers made the best of what they had. Like brothers in a family they shared their meals and did their best. It was a lesson that even in the most challenging of situations we too can become much tougher than we imagine when we work together.

In the trenches the soldiers had to be on constant alert to enemy attacks. Explosions and gunfire constantly rang around them making it difficult to find a moment of peace. Furthermore, they faced harsh weather conditions from heavy rains, to freezing winters, to the sweltering heat of summer. Despite these challenges they showed incredible strength, brotherhood and determination. Together they became like a team of superheroes supporting each other through the tough times. Unbreakable bonds were formed and they stood by each other to protect their countries with honour and bravery.

In a way trench life was a never-ending adventure. But it wasn't the normal adventure filled with fun but rather it was filled with hardship and sacrifice. Many of the soldiers in the trenches were young men far away from home surrounded by unfamiliar faces in foreign lands. They missed their family, friends and the comforts of home. Back in those days they didn't have Wi-Fi, messenger or email. So how did they stay in contact with loved ones back at home?

During World War 1 letters were written that connected soldiers to their loved ones. Soldiers wrote heartfelt letters to their families to share their experiences, their hopes and their fears. In the muddy trenches they would write by the dim light of a lantern light. They would write home to their loved ones about how much they missed them and the difficulties they were facing. Every letter was like sending a little bit of themselves across the world. Families sent their own letters in return to the soldiers providing strength and love to them. These letters were more than just words on paper. They were the lifeblood of family relationships and a fuel for hope in desperate times. Those letters serve as a reminder that despite the horrors of war, human connection, compassion, and understanding can make us stronger than ever. Soldiers also wrote down their thoughts and feelings in journals. Many of the details we know about life in the trenches come from these diaries. The pages, which were like a time capsule, were written on by young soldiers and preserved their memories, emotions, and experiences from the trenches.

Trench warfare strategies

Trench warfare used various strategies to gain an

advantage in this gruelling type of combat. Here are some of the most famous strategies.

- Trench raids

  Under the cover of night, groups of soldiers would sneak into enemy trenches to launch surprise attacks. The attacks had to be executed with stealth, bravery and speed.

- Artillery barrages

  Artillery barrages were a powerful move that sought to weaken the opponent's defences. Imagine a stack of guns unleashing devastating rounds of bullets onto enemy positions. These barrages filled the air with chaos and destruction which would create openings for infantry assaults.

- Gas attacks

  Gas attacks were an unfortunate reality of trench warfare. Deadly gases like chlorine and mustard gas rolled across the land choking and blinding soldiers in their pathway. Gas attacks disrupted plans and caused terror in the trenches.

- Infantry charges

  Soldiers would charge across "no man's land" in an act of bravery. On the battlefield, this area served as a physical barrier between those fighting. Mines, bullets and shrapnel whizzed past soldiers as they pushed forward to overrun enemy trenches. It was a high-stakes strategy with a high potential payoff. But it also carried a high probability of failure.

- Tunnelling and mining

  Soldiers would dig deep beneath enemy lines to plant explosives underneath the enemy. But this was a dangerous game of cat and mouse. If they were detected then they would face devastating consequences.

Innovations in trench warfare

There were numerous developments made in the trenches. Some of the most crucial ones are summarised below. A more detailed list can be found at the end of this book.

- Gas masks
  When gas warfare became a major part of the war, gas masks were invented to shield and protect soldiers from the deadly attacks. First they evolved from simple cloth masks to more sophisticated designs to offer life saving protection.

- Periscopes
  Periscopes allowed soldiers to see the enemy from the safety of their own trenches. This provided valuable information without exposing the soldiers to bullets.

- Flamethrowers
  Flamethrowers were like mythical dragons launching fire across the battlefields. In a blast they could clear enemy troops with terrifying efficiency. However, holding one took courage as the operator would often be a target for enemy snipers.

- Tanks
  Tanks could steamroll across the battlefield navigating rough terrain and providing firepower. Enemy lines were easily crushed underneath them. The appearance of tanks marked a major shift in battlefield dynamics.

- Barb wire
  Barb wire was used as a defence around the trenches to keep away enemies. Those unfortunate enough to be

wrapped up in the jagged edges would be stuck in the sights of enemy fire.

In this chapter you learned about the grim realities of trench warfare. Remember the courage and bravery of the soldiers who fought for their nations in foreign muddy and dangerous lands. In the next chapter we will learn all about the heroes back home who supported them. (Bull, 2002)

A soldier writing letters in the trenches

CHAPTER 4
HOME FRONT HEROES

Welcome back once again young historians! So far on our trip through time, we've visited the front lines of World War 1 and studied some truly remarkable people who risked their lives to save others. Now we'll take flight to the home front, where unsung heroes, women and kids your age played a crucial role in the war effort.

Take a moment to think about what you do every single day. You probably wake up, go to school, have some lunch, do your homework and then relax with your friends and family. Back in the days of World War 1 kids your age also followed a similar routine. But when the war began everything changed in the blink of an eye. Parents were called away to fight in foreign lands. Meanwhile back in the homelands children just like you stepped up in extraordinary ways to support their countries and their country people fighting overseas. On the home front, they established themselves as a reliable support system for the war effort. As you're about to see, they also showed remarkable resourcefulness and determination.

Young heroes at home

During World War 1, there were many young people who stood up and helped with the war effort. Firstly they contributed to the collection of essentials like clothing, blankets and even soap. Even though they seemed like small contributions, they made a huge difference to helping the soldiers endure the harsh conditions of the war. Conditions for soldiers on the front lines were often dangerous and harsh. The bitter winter weather constantly bit at them. But the heroes at the home fronts worked diligently to create cosy socks and warm scarves. With determination and care they knitted these warm items for the soldiers fighting far away from home. With each stitch sewn it was a symbol of support and a reminder that there was someone back home thinking of them.

Remember that such simple acts of kindness can have a big impact. These young heroes proved that you don't need to be a superhero or wear a cape to make a difference. Even the smallest actions and teamwork can help to make positive changes. Through community, compassion and determination they helped the soldiers overseas to stay strong. All together their actions even though they seemed small played a significant role in helping their countries and the soldiers on the front lines. Allow their stories to inspire you to always see opportunities to lend a helping hand in challenging situations. Every effort no matter how small can contribute to a greater cause and make the world a better place.

Young spies

In times of war information is one of the most valuable weapons. When you know your enemies strategies and secrets it can help to unlock the keys to victory. Spies can help to gather important information that can help win wars. With their smart and cunning skills they can sneak behind enemy lines to gather intelligence and uncover hidden secrets. Can you imagine being a spy? It wasn't easy, and it was very nerve racking. You constantly had to be two steps ahead of the enemy in a bid to outsmart them.

Did you know that back in World War 1 some of the most daring spies were kids? Indeed many were not much older than you! Of course being young and innocent made them the perfect undercover agents because they were less likely to raise suspicion. Now let's take a look at some of the ways that they spied on the enemies.

On daring missions they risked being captured whilst gathering information. At all times they had to be quick thinkers and adapt to many unexpected situations. Many times they had to use all their resourcefulness to escape the stickiest of situations. Each mission was like a puzzle and solving them required a sharp mind combined with courage. They were like characters from a thrilling adventure novel but this was the real world. They had to be masters of disguise, quickly able to take on various identities of newsboys, messengers or even students

Taking pictures was an important way of gathering information during the war. Young spies photographed sensitive information about the enemy. These young spies would sneak up on enemy troops and locations by posing as newsboys or messengers. Then they would send back extremely useful visual intelligence captured by their cameras.

Another important tactic these young spies were involved in was breaking codes. Together they joined forces with other code breakers to decipher enemy messages. The ability of young minds to decipher codes and solve puzzles was remarkable. Their nations were able to better intercept and decipher enemy communications thanks to the data they gathered.

Remember that you too have a sharp mind and a courageous character. Master your skills and work hard on becoming the best you can be. When the time comes you too will face challenges but with your experience and knowledge you'll easily overcome them.

Children on the home front

During World War I, young people organised various groups to show unity with the armed forces and their communities.These clubs and adventures were more than just having fun; they were about making a positive impact on the home front.

Meet Olivia, an eleven year old girl who founded a kids for kindness club in her school. Her club was all about focusing on acts of kindness in the form of writing letters to the soldiers and to help neighbours in need. Her club became a symbol of hope and a helping hand within the community that lifted the peoples spirits.

Meet Daniel, a fourteen year old boy who organised the bicycle brigade. Kids in his gang rode their bicycles to collect donations for the soldiers fighting overseas. Together they peddled through the streets and the parks spreading the gifts of generosity everywhere they went. On their journeys they helped to raise spirits and important funds for the soldiers fighting overseas.

Youths like Olivia and Daniel proved that with creativity and determination young people in the community can become leaders and make a difference. Keep in mind that kids your age can be powerful forces for good as we continue to learn about the lives of our home front heroes. You too can make a difference in the world by doing something as simple as fixing something, starting a club or helping someone else.

Women in the war

At the start of World War 1 women were involved in the traditional roles such as staying at home to take care of children and to perform regular home tasks. However as the war became more intense it became very clear that more help would be required. Luckily women were there to help!

One of the most important roles women played during World War 1 was nurses. Bravely those women who were often called "the angels of the battlefield" served on the front lines. There they tended to wounded soldiers with compassion and care. Tirelessly they worked in the field hospitals and risked their lives to save others. With dedication and resilience they bravely faced unimaginable horrors to complete their duties. Without them things would have been much worse and it was with gratitude that their efforts were received.

Whilst some women worked as nurses others took on equally important roles such as ambulance drivers and medics. Bravely they faced the dangers of the battlefield to bring back injured soldiers for medical treatment. Courageously these women navigated through dangerous conditions to save lives.

Beyond the medical field women also served as spies and code breakers. With their sharp minds they proved to be valuable at gathering important information and cracking enemy codes. We will never know their names because they worked in secret but their impactful efforts made a big difference.

Not all women served on the front lines but many more played an important role in the war. Back on the home front many women played crucial roles such as taking jobs at factories, offices and farms allowing the men who previously worked there to head off to war. The women who remained home took great care to preserve a strong home front and allow the war efforts to continue.

Women in World War 1 became an important part of our history. Before then they were not treated equally. The war proved that they too are just as capable as men. After the war in many countries women gained the right to vote and became more active in society and politics. Their stories from World War 1 serve as a reminder that strength and resilience regardless of gender can shape the course of history. Not only did they save lives but they also set the stage for a more equal and inclusive future. The legacy of these women is a testament to the power and determination of breaking down barriers. Always treat each other with fairness regardless of their background. Our merits and efforts are what make us and create opportunities for us.

Now the stage has been set and the heroes have been met. It's time for us to venture out into some of the major battles of World War 1. (Storey & Housego, 2010)

Women and children
on the homefront

PART TWO:
MAJOR BATTLES

CHAPTER 5
WESTERN FRONT
1914 TO 1916

W elcome to a new thrilling part of our journey through the history of World War 1. Here we are about to enter the first battles of the war. Imagine a massive battlefield that covered most of Europe. Here, huge armies would fight fierce and decisive battles in a bid to win the war. In these early battles history was shaped in the fires of war.

At the beginning of World War 1, things got pretty confusing for the Central Powers. They had a plan. But it didn't quite work out the way they expected. Germany had promised to help Austria-Hungary attack Serbia. However each side had a different idea of what that help should look like. Before the war, the Central Powers had made some plans on how to fight, but they didn't go as expected. When the war started it was like they were playing a game without knowing the rules!

Austria-Hungary thought that Germany would protect

them from Russia in the north. But Germany thought Austria-Hungary would focus on fighting Russia while they took care of France in the west. It was like they were speaking different languages! This confusion caused Austria-Hungary to send its soldiers to both the Russian and Serbian sides. Overall this would make things even more confusing and challenging for the Central Powers.

The Serbian Adventure

On August 12th, something major happened in the land of Serbia. Austrian and Serb forces fought battles at a place called Cer and another one at a place called Kolubara. These battles lasted for about two weeks. The Austrians hoped for a quick victory, but it didn't work out that way because the Serbs put up such a strong resistance. The news disappointed the Austrians. The Serbs' ability to stop the Austrians was a big surprise and one of the first times the countries on the Allies won a big fight in the war. Because of this, the Austrians had to keep many soldiers in Serbia, which made it tough for them to fight against Russia. (Lyon, 2015)

Something interesting also happened during this Serbian adventure. In the spring of 1915, they used special guns to shoot down an Austrian aeroplane. That was the first time anyone had done that in a war. And later in the fall of 1915 something else amazing happened. The Serbian forces made a superhero move, where they helped many injured soldiers by saving them from the fighting zones. (Miller et al., 2009)

The Big German march

Back in 1914, the German army had a plan to quickly take over Belgium and France. With many of their soldiers lined up and ready on the Western Front, they hatched a special plan called the Schlieffen Plan. Their leader, Alfred von Schlieffen, thought that they could surprise the other side by going through the Netherlands and Belgium. His plan was to then sweep down and trap the French army near Switzerland. Ideally, this would take no more than six weeks. From then they could head east to fight Russia.

But, there was a problem. After Schlieffen, another leader named Helmuth von Moltke made some changes to the plan. He was worried that the French might be too strong on the left side. Thus he moved some soldiers there. Also, he decided not to go through the Netherlands because he wanted to keep them friendly for trade. (Foley, 2012)

The Germans began their march and did really well at first. They even made some of the Allied forces, including the British retreat. But, then the French launched a counter attack in a place called Alsace-Lorraine. It didn't go well for them and they lost many soldiers which turned the tides. As the Germans got closer to Paris they made a mistake. One of their commanders, von Kluck, didn't follow orders which created a gap between their armies. The French and the British saw this gap and stopped the German advance at a place called the First Battle of the Marne. (Herwig, 2009)

By the end of 1914, the German soldiers were deep inside France. They were doing okay and had taken control of some important places. However they had problems with talking to each other and some leaders made some bad decisions. They were also being challenged to fight the Russians in the east. This meant they had to send important soldiers away from France to deal with the Russians. Some people in Germany already knew they were in trouble and thought they might lose the war, even though it was just beginning.

Tough times on the front lines

When World War 1 started, the way armies fought had to change. Before then soldiers used to fight in open fields with their rifles. But in 1914, things were changing because new technology made it really hard to do that. The introduction of barbed wire, machine guns and powerful artillery made it tougher for soldiers to fight in open fields. Battlefields had become like giant obstacle courses. For a while, neither side knew how to break through these defences without losing many soldiers in their efforts. But as time went on new weapons like gas and tanks began to change the game.

After the First Battle of the Marne, the Allies and the Germans tried to outflank each other, which meant going around the sides to surprise the enemy. They called this the "Race to the Sea." But by the end of 1914, they couldn't go any further and they had to stop. They stood facing each other with trenches and barbed wire all the way from the sea to the Swiss border.

The Germans usually held the higher ground and had stronger trenches because they got to pick where they stood. The French and English trenches weren't as good at first because they built them thinking they would only be temporary. Their plan had always been to break through the German defences as quickly as possible.

In 1915, during the Second Battle of Ypres, the Germans did something really scary. They used a poisonous gas called chlorine for the first time in a war. From then onwards both sides began using different gases. This was a scary new element of war that had dire consequences. Along with tanks and innovation the game of war began to change. (Leach, 2016)

For the next two years, neither side could win the war. The British and French lost more soldiers than the Germans because of the ways they tried to attack. The Germans only launched one big attack, but the Allies made many attempts to break through the German lines.

In 1916, there was a famous battle called the Battle of Verdun where the Germans tried to capture land, but the French fought back with full effort. Many soldiers from both sides got hurt and it ultimately became a symbol of how determined the French were. (Jankowski, 2014)

Later that year, there was another big battle called the Battle of the Somme. The first day of this battle was the deadliest day in British Army history. Many soldiers were either hurt or killed. Overall the battle led to many casualties on all sides. Not only did gunshots hurt, but life in the trenches was really bad. Diseases like trench foot, shell shock, and the 'Spanish flu' made many soldiers sick. It was a tough time for everyone on the front lines. (Prior & Wilson, 2016)

As we close the pages of Chapter 5, we have ventured deep into the trenches of World War 1, where we've witnessed the relentless struggles, battles and suffering endured by the brave soldiers. However our exploration of this moment in time remains far from complete.

For now we will bid farewell to the muddy trenches. Next we are about to set sail into uncharted waters. Our next voyage will navigate the seas of naval warfare, where mighty warships, sneaky submarines and strategic manoeuvres would come to define the course of World War 1.

The Battle of Somme

CHAPTER 6
FIGHTING FOR CONTROL
OF THE SEAS

We've already learned a great deal about the trenches of World War 1. However our journey through time is still early on! In this next chapter, we'll board onto ships, head out to sea and discover a new front in the naval conflict. In this chapter, we'll set sail for a study of the great naval battles, vessels and legacies of World War 1. Prepare yourself to navigate the dangerous waters of this historic period where ships, submarines and strategic moves shaped the course of the war.

Imagine a huge competition on the high seas. But this wasn't about sports or games. No this was about something much more important! It was a race between countries to build the most powerful fleet of warships. The two leading contenders were the Royal Navy of the United Kingdom and the Imperial Navy of Germany. Huge battles between these sea monsters took place on the choppy seas. In these battles, warships on the water were crucial whilst submarines were used for secret surveillance and stealthy attacks.

A brief Naval history background

A long time ago, a leader named Wilhelm wanted his country, Germany, to have a powerful navy like the one in Britain. He really looked up to the British navy and wanted to be even stronger than them. He thought that if Germany had a strong navy, the British wouldn't bother Germany in Europe. In the meantime, Britain completed construction of the super-advanced ship HMS Dreadnought. Germany made an immense effort to catch up but it was tough. This was the general mood back when countries were competing to build the strongest navies. (Hamilton, 2004)

The Battle of Jutland

When World War 1 began at sea, the Battle of Jutland was one of the first and most famous battles. Everything went down in the North Sea, not far from the coasts of Denmark and Northwest Germany. Several countries, including the United Kingdom to the west and Denmark, Norway, Sweden, and Germany to the east, surrounded the North Sea. Imagine a vast, cold and deep sea that stretches as far as your eyes can see. The scene was set for a naval battle of legendary size.

The British Grand Fleet, commanded by Admiral Sir John Jellico, made up one side. The ships under his command were like floating fortresses, armed to the teeth with massive cannons. Facing them on the other side was the Imperial German High Seas Fleet commanded by Admiral Reinhard Scheer. Under his command was a fleet of German warships that were equally impressive with their own powerful weapons. As these two mighty navies faced each other, the North Sea was about to witness a dramatic clash.

Now imagine the North Sea as a massive chessboard. Each

warship represented a powerful chess piece. The German and British Admirals were like grand chess masters planning their moves against each other with precision. On the afternoon of May 31, 1916, combat began. Each side was making strategic moves in the opening stages, much like a chess game. The British strategy was to line up their ships to "cross the T", a move that would direct their cannons at the enemy.

Darkness fell over the ocean as the sun set. Suddenly, the sky was lit up by the battle. Sounds of gunfire echoed through the night. The sky lit up with cannon fire like a fireworks show. Scenes of chaos and destruction were created as shells screamed through the air and crashed into the ships as the ocean caught fire.

Midnight approached and the battle reached a climatic moment. The British Grand Fleet executed a daring manoeuvre to "cross the T" of the German Seas fleet. Executed like a brilliant chess move, it put the British in a dominant position. Suddenly the Germans realised that they were in serious danger and so they skillfully retreated into the cover of darkness. The British Grand Fleet held the advantage but the Germans had managed to escape without suffering a devastating defeat.

The Battle of Jutland was a brutal, intense clash that lasted for hours. When the smoke finally cleared and dawn broke both sides claimed their own victories. Whilst the British had caused more damage to the Germans, their high seas fleet had also taken some damage. Ultimately the battle didn't provide a decisive victory for either side but it did have profound consequences. The British had proved to be effective at blocking Germany and slowly choking off its vital supplies. Meanwhile the Germans had demonstrated resilience. (Brooks, 2016)

The Battle of Jutland changed the course of World War 1 in many ways. It caused the German high seas fleet to rethink engaging in open conflict and instead concentrate on submarine warfare. Inevitably, this would lead to events like the sinking of the British steamship Lusitania by a German U-boat. This claimed the lives of both British and American citizens. These U-boats had tried to stop ships from bringing supplies to Britain from North America. Sneakily they would attack ships without any warning. This was really scary for the people on those ships because they didn't have much time to escape. The United States got upset about this and told Germany it wasn't fair. So, Germany changed its rules and promised not to attack passenger ships. But Britain did something different. They put guns on their merchant ships and didn't give a warning before firing.

Things started getting better for the ships in 1917 when they started travelling together in groups called convoys with destroyers to protect them. This made it hard for the U-boats to find and attack the ships and it helped reduce the number of ships that got sunk. They also came up with new ways to find and fight the U-boats underwater. It was like a game of hide and seek, but with submarines and special weapons. During this time, they also started using aeroplanes on big ships called aircraft carriers. These aeroplanes helped them attack important places such as aircraft hangars. They even used blimps to look for U-boats underwater. (Gray, 1994)

Ultimately it was a tough time at sea during World War 1. Many lives were lost and many ships were destroyed. Let us pay respect and remember the bravery and sacrifice of all involved. Now we will venture into Chapter 7 where fresh adventures, challenges and shifting alliances await.

Ships at war in The Battle of Jutland

CHAPTER 7
FRESH CHALLENGES & SOUTHERN THEATRES

As our journey continues deeper into the story of World War 1 we now find ourselves exploring new battlefields. New threats, rivals, enemies and alliances were beginning to emerge. One such challenge was beginning in the heart of Europe where Austria-Hungary faced a massive challenge. Back in those days Austria-Hungary ruled over a vast empire that included many different countries. However they were on the verge of collapse from the weight of their many commitments and limited resources.

After the assassination of Archduke Franz Ferdinand at the hands of a terrorist supported by Serbia, Austria-Hungary was driven to assert its superiority. In an effort to crush Serbian nationalism, Austria-Hungary decided to punish the country. Germany and Austria-Hungary formed a powerful team in this battle. Together they convinced another country Bulgaria to join them in battle against Serbia. Bulgaria when they were asked to join in didn't hesitate, they quickly said "count us in".

On October 14th 1915 Bulgaria declared war on Serbia. Together they joined forces with the Austrian-Hungarian army which was already in the midst of a huge attack involving over six hundred thousand soldiers. Serbia was faced with a tough challenge. Now they had to fight on two sides. The odds were stacked against them and defeat seemed imminent. With all their might they fought against the massive Austria-Hungarian and Bulgarian armies. (Hall, 2014)

The Serbs tried really hard, but they were pushed back towards the sea. In another battle called the Battle of Mojkovac, their friends from Montenegro helped them. But even that didn't work. The Austrians took over Montenegro too. The Serbian soldiers who were left had to escape by sea to Greece or by land into Albania in the south.

Ultimately they were faced with overwhelming forces. Despite their heroic efforts, they just couldn't hold on to their land. The combined strength of the Bulgarian and Austrian-Hungarian armies was just too much. After falling, Serbia was then occupied and divided between the Austro-Hungarian Empire and Bulgaria. However we will revisit them later to see how they came back from the dead.

Troubles in Greece

Now let's hop over to Greece which was a neighbouring country with its own share of troubles during this chaotic time. Remember the Allies? Well this super team of countries including France and the United Kingdom wanted to help Greece in the war because they believed it would make a big difference. However there was a hitch in the plan.

King Constantine 1 of Greece was good friends with Germany of The Central Powers. When the Allies asked for

Greece's support the king wasn't so keen on the idea. So instead of teaming up with the Allies he decided to follow his own path which didn't involve joining them. Like a storm on the horizon, an explosive argument erupted over it. As tensions rose, the people of Greece were now split into two camps. One who supported the king, while the other who sided with the Allies.

The clash between the Allies and the king's forces escalated and it eventually led to an armed confrontation in the heart of the Greek capital, Athens. This dramatic event is now remembered as Noemvriana. The king, feeling the heat, decided to step down from his throne and was succeeded by his son Alexander in June 1917. Greece now officially joined with the Allies.

With Greece now siding with the Allies the balance was shifting. It was a significant moment in the history of World War 1 which would have far reaching consequences. So dear readers hold on to your hats as we enter further into the epic tale of this global conflict. There's so much more to learn and as you'll soon find out the war was spreading far and wide. (Abbott, 2022)

Macedonia

Now, let's travel to a place called Macedonia. In the beginning of World War 1, the fight in Macedonia didn't move much. But then, something important happened. A group of brave French and Serbian soldiers decided to take over a town called Bitola in November 1916. It was a really tough battle and it cost them a lot. But they didn't give up and they managed to capture Bitola. This made things a little calmer for a while and it was like a small victory in the middle of a big war.

The most exciting part came in September 1918. By this

time, most of the bad guys from Germany and Austria had left the fight. The Bulgarians, who were on the bad side, got defeated in a big battle called Dobro Pole. And by September 25, British and French soldiers had even gone into Bulgaria itself because the Bulgarian army was falling apart. Just four days later, on September 29, Bulgaria said they couldn't fight anymore. (Hall, 2010)

The Germans tried to send more soldiers to stop them, but they were too weak to fight back. With the fight in Macedonia settled, the way to two big cities, Budapest and Vienna, was now open for the Allies. The Central Powers knew they couldn't win anymore, so they decided to make peace. More on that later but for now let's meet another big player in the war.

Italy joins the show

Italy faced a tough choice to make in the early days of World War 1. Like a referee on the sidelines of a soccer game, they first had no motivation to get involved. The Italian government declared neutrality at the outbreak of war, but public opinion was divided at the time. The war went on for a lot longer and grew much larger than anyone had expected. As the war progressed it was rapidly approaching its borders and Italy was starting to feel anxious.

In the early years, Italy had signed a secret deal with Germany and Austria-Hungary prior to World War 1. However, when things escalated, they decided they could no longer stick to this deal. They decided that Austria-Hungary was being overly aggressive. Disputes over Austro-Hungarian territory where Italian was spoken also played a role. Italy had always asserted its right to rule over those territories and the Allies had promised Italy these territories in exchange for their help. Public opinion began to turn in favour of the Allies.

Furthermore the risks of doing nothing became clearer to Italy, so the country prepared for war.

When World War 1 began, the Italians thought it was a good chance to make their country stronger. They joined the Allies, because they believed it would help them achieve their dream of a united and stronger Italy. Italy's economy was also struggling at the time. They hoped to increase their wealth through international trade. Italy's entry into the war allowed the country to form alliances with other nations, which would boost economic growth after the conflict ended. As a result, many Italians saw joining the war as part of a grand strategy to expand and enrich their nation. They hoped it would improve their negotiating position with foreign nations and make them even more awesome.

Italy had a well-developed military by the time it entered the war in 1915. After careful consideration, Italy chose to join the war on the side that had the best chance of winning. It became clear that the Allies were gaining ground and Italy seized the opportunity to join the victorious coalition as the war dragged on. Their involvement changed the nature of the war and had far-reaching effects on both their own history and the final outcome of World War 1.

Battles on the Italian Front

Now it's time for us to enter into the stunning landscapes of the Italian front. This front ran through the beautiful Italian Alps, a region with a long and storied military history. Close your eyes and imagine this place filled with rugged mountain peaks and deep valleys where soldiers travelled through the treacherous trains. The Italian front quickly developed into a busy battleground where both sides fought for power. Time travellers, let's begin our trip to the Italian front of World War 1.

The Italian Front was a new front that formed in the Alpine region after Italy joined the Allies in May 1915. Picture a fierce battle taking place among the jagged peaks of the Alps, with Italian soldiers in their olive green uniforms. The battles on this front involved high stakes games of outwitting and outmanoeuvring the enemy. The stunning yet unforgiving landscapes served as the backdrop for the stories of bravery and sacrifice, from the bloody Battle of Caporetto to the heroic defence at the Battle of Monte Grappa. (Marcuzzi, 2020)

The battles on the Italian front were long and brutal. Many resulted in prolonged stalemates that ultimately contributed to wearing down the Central Powers. In addition it took a huge economic strain on all forces involved. The cost of building armies and bases in challenging terrains drained resources that could have been used for other purposes. The Italian front was a unique moment in World War 1 where the soldiers weren't just fighting the enemy but they were battling the elements as well. They were faced with snow covered peaks, icy winds, avalanches and dangerous enemies. In mountain warfare frostbite and altitude sickness were just as deadly as the enemy's bullets. Not only did they face dangerous enemies but they also faced survival in some of the world's most challenging conditions. The mountainous terrain of the Italian Front was a unique challenge for both sides. It required vast resources for building bases, supply lines and sending troops to the mountains where that had to acclimatise. This drain on resources was a problem for both Italy and Austria-Hungary and it had greater consequences in the balance of power of the war.

As a result of Italy's entry into the conflict, the Central Powers, led by Austria-Hungary, were forced to redirect an enormous amount of their military and resources toward securing their southern borders. However, the military forces of these countries were already being put to heavy use on the Eastern and Western Fronts. Now they had to split those forces to face the Italians. Because of this, Austria-Hungary was put under tremendous pressure as it had to defend a difficult terrain from Italian attacks. The Central Powers could have used those resources elsewhere, but strengthening the Italian Front was a must. As a result, the Central Powers' strategy was weakened and Austria-Hungary was unable to launch massive attacks elsewhere. Ultimately, it swung the odds in favour of the Allies and tipped the balance of power to them. The Central Powers' isolation was deepened as a new powerful ally in Italy joined against their coalition.

Soldiers in The Alps

CHAPTER 8
THE OTTOMAN EMPIRE

• • • • • • • • • •

As the war progressed, it covered new territories and drew in additional countries. With World War 1 as a backdrop, this chapter will now take us into the fascinating world of the Ottoman Empire, where alliances shifted and battles for control unfolded. For more than six centuries, the Ottoman Empire had ruled over a vast territory. Located at the crossroads of Europe, Asia and Africa it was a significant player in the history of the world. It was really, really huge and covered three continents! In Europe it included southeastern Europe with territories in the Balkans and Greece. In Asia most of the empire was located in modern day Turkey, regions of the middle East and parts of western Asia. Even in Africa parts of the empire were located in Libya, Egypt and Sudan.

Historical Background

The Ottoman Empire originated in the early 14th century when it was founded by Osman 1 from whom the Empire took its name. Originally it emerged from the Byzantine Empire and over time expanded through military conquests, diplomacy and strategic alliances. As the centuries passed it became one of the most powerful and legendary empires in history. (Editors, 2019)

In the early years of World War 1 the Ottoman Empire was led by the ambitious leadership of the Young Turks. The Young Turks wanted to replace the Ottoman Empire's absolute monarchy with a new constitutional government. A turning point in its history occurred during World War 1. Initially taking a neutral stance, the Ottoman Empire ultimately joined forces with Germany and Austria-Hungary to form The Central Powers. But it would end up being a bad decision with far-reaching consequences. (Turfan, 2000)

Gallipoli Campaign

Now let's get on a boat and head to the beautiful Ottoman Peninsula of Gallipoli. The sea and the past meet at this point in time. The Allies, which included forces from Australia and New Zealand, were plotting an assault against The Central Powers in the Ottoman Empire. Soldiers in this campaign would undertake a daring mission, storming beaches and crossing perilous cliffs and trenches.

Brave soldiers from Australia and New Zealand embarked on a daring adventure to break the stalemate that had gripped the Western Front for so long. Like knights in shining armour they stepped into the unknown with the hope of turning the tides of war in their favour. But it would come at a great cost. The Gallipoli Peninsula was a dangerous and rocky terrain protected by fierce and determined Ottoman defenders.

In April 1915 the daring and audacious plan began to unfold. Allied forces including the Australian and New Zealand corps (ANZAC) embarked on an ambitious, amphibious assault on The Gallipoli Peninsula. Their mission was to secure the beaches and establish a foothold in a place that was filled with uncertainty and challenges. This presented significant challenges from the beginning. (McLean, 2009)

The Gallipoli Peninsula was a rugged and rocky landscape that made it incredibly difficult for troops to move through. Rocky shores and steep cliffs added to the complexity of their assault. Furthermore, the Ottomans had put up a fierce defence under the leadership of Mustafa Kemal Atatürk, later the founder of modern Turkey. His forces had been sent to the Peninsula with determination to protect their homeland. Against them The Allies also had to contend with harsh weather conditions ranging from scorching heat in the summer to the bitter cold of the winter. Combined with limited resources and supplies it proved to be a very difficult task.

Despite initial successes the campaign soon became a long drawn out challenge resulting in a stalemate. Both sides found themselves in a situation that was becoming worse by the day. The ANZAC troops alongside the British and the French endured unimaginable conditions and suffered heavy casualties. In some situations they were even involved in brutal hand-to-hand combat. The Gallipoli campaign became a symbol of courage and determination. Both sides showed incredible bravery in the face of adversity earning the respect and admiration of their comrades.

The campaign dragged on for eight long months and neither side was able to secure a victory. By December 1915 the Allied forces saw the futility of the situation and decided to evacuate from The Gallipoli. For the Ottoman Empire the successful defence of their terrain against foreign invasion contributed to the eventual foundation of modern Turkey. Mustafa Kemal Atatürk's leadership would become a defining chapter in that history. The Gallipoli campaign ultimately remains a powerful chapter in the history of World War 1 marked by valour, sacrifice and the memories of those who fell on its rocky shores.

The Armenian Genocide

As we continue our journey through time, we will learn more about the Ottoman Empire's involvement in World War 1. The Armenian Genocide is a tragic chapter in the history of human suffering that we must now confront.

Armenia was a land of rich culture and heritage. Located in the South Caucasus region of Western Asia deep within the Ottoman Empire. In modern day terms it was nestled between Turkey to the west, Georgia to the north, Azerbaijan to the east and Iran to the South. Armenia has a long history that stretches back thousands of years with significant contributions to art, literature and religion.

Now let us turn our attention to this deeply sombre chapter in the history of the Armenian people. This chapter unfolded within the borders of the Ottoman Empire where a shadow descended upon the Armenian population. It was a shadow of cruelty and suffering that was a stark contrast to the vibrant culture these people had celebrated for generations.

The Armenian Genocide was a heart-wrenching tail of tragedy where mass deportations, violence and suffering took place. It was as though a hurricane had swept through those peoples lives pushing out families from their homes, tearing apart communities and subjecting innocent individuals to unimaginable hardships.

Families were forcibly separated, their homes were taken over and their lives were forever changed. Armenians who had long been a treasured part of the Ottoman Empire's diverse culture were treated as outcasts and were either thrown out or killed. But why?

Several factors contributed to the Armenian Genocide. The Armenians were a distinct Christian minority in a predominantly Muslim Ottoman Empire. This created a religious divide that had long and complicated historical roots. As the Ottoman Empire struggled with internal strife and territorial losses a sense of nationalism grew amongst ethnic groups.

The Armenian population was seen as a potential threat due to their ethnic identity and aspirations for autonomy. Furthermore the Ottoman Empire during World War 1 wanted to secure its eastern borderlands and prevent potential collaborations between the Armenians and the Ottoman Empire's enemies such as Russia. Ultimately World War 1 ignited the tensions even more and as the war waged on, the Ottoman Empire engaged in mass deportations, violence and atrocities against the Armenian population. The enduring lessons from this chapter serve as a harsh reminder to the horrors that can unfold when hatred and intolerance are allowed to flourish unchecked. As seekers of knowledge and historians we must learn from it and work towards a better future. (Kévorkian, 2011)

As the war dragged on the Ottoman Empire continued to face internal strife as well as external threats. Forevermore its roots had been weakened by World War 1. Ultimately this had set in motion its eventual collapse and the birth of new nations in its wake.

*Mustafa Kemal Atatürk,
founder of Modern Turkey*

CHAPTER 9
ADVENTURES IN THE EAST: HEROES, CHANGES, AND BIG BATTLES

The next stop on our tour across the battlefields of World War 1 lands us in Eastern Europe. More players were about to enter into the action. In this chapter, we will learn about Romania's role in World War 1, the consequences and other important moments on the Eastern Front. Moreover, we'll bear witness to the emergence of the colossal Russian giant, whose entry into the war would forever alter the course of history.

Picture the vast region of Eastern Europe as the backdrop, where the Carpathian Mountains stand tall like giants and the Danube River flows fast and furiously. It's here that we will uncover the remarkable story of Romania's brave soldiers, who stepped onto the world stage with hopes of making their mark. We'll follow their battles and the impact they had on a complicated network of alliances and rivalries.

The Eastern front of World War 1 expanded far across Eastern Europe. Picture a map of Europe and visualise a line that stretches from the Baltic Sea in the north to the Black Sea in the south. This line represented the front line of the Eastern Front and it is a region that included modern-day Poland, Ukraine, Belarus, the Baltic states, Russia and Romania. Military operations in the region were complicated by the wide variety of languages and cultures there.

Close your eyes and imagine this landscape that ranges from the sweeping planes of Russia to the rugged Carpathian mountains of the Czech Republic to Romania. Armies were tasked with manoeuvring through thick forests, crossing mighty rivers and enduring harsh winters. Nations sought to protect their interests, assert their dominance and emerge victorious in the shifting alliances of World War 1.

Romania

Romania, a country in Eastern Europe, faced a crucial decision in 1916, during World War 1. Two choices lay before them. Option one was to team up with the Allies, a group of friendly countries like the United Kingdom, France and Russia. These friends promised Romania land and help. Option two was to join the Central Powers, led by Germany and Austria-Hungary, who they were once friendly with. Romania's leaders thought really hard and decided to go with the Allies. This was unusual because it meant they became friends with the countries they used to be against. Such a choice was a big deal and it would change things for Romania in many ways.

Romania's borders became a big battlefield in the game of war. Romanian soldiers went on special missions during the big battles. One mission involved saving a place called Transylvania, where many Romanians lived. But guess what?

Hungary, part of a place called the Austro-Hungarian empire, controlled it. Romanian soldiers were super brave. They climbed mountains and fought really hard to help their people in Transylvania. It was tough, but they didn't give up. Their courage showed how strong they were and it made a big difference.

Another frontline opened in Moldova where Romanian forces faced large armies from the Central Powers. On the banks of the Siret and Prut rivers fierce battles were fought as Romania defended its territory and stuck by their commitment to the Allied cause. The Siret and Prut rivers served as national boundaries and defensive positions for Romanian forces. Along these waterways Romanian soldiers displayed a brave determination to protect their homelands.

The Central Powers, meanwhile, were making moves to strengthen their control over important territory and assets in the area. The fighting along this front line became especially fierce and difficult. Extreme weather, a lack of supplies, and the constant fear of enemy attacks were just some of the many challenges faced by soldiers on both sides. The bravery and perseverance of those who fought on this front, as well as the suffering of those who lived nearby became legendary.

Eastern Europe became a complicated chessboard of shifting alliances and ambitions after Romania's full entry into the war. The already tense historical situation in the region was further complicated by joining the Allies. Ultimately their involvement in the war had a significant effect on the Eastern Front. As a result of strong rivals led by Russia on the Eastern Front, the Central Powers were weakened as they were forced to shift more resources from the Western Front. Forced to devote troops and resources, the Central Powers' Romanian campaign altered the regional balance of power in Eastern Europe.

As we move forward in our exploration of World War 1, it is crucial that we never forget the contributions of countries like Romania. Those who fought on the front lines and helped at home were crucial in turning the tide of the war. (Torrey, 1998)

Russia

One of the defining features of the Eastern Front was the massive mobilisation of the Russian Empire. Imagine a massive bear emerging from a long sleep. This was kind of how it felt when thousands of Russian soldiers were awakened from their sleep. During the height of the Russian Empire's recruitment drive and because of its massive population, Russia was able to build huge armies. Ultimately this would be a game changer.

But why did Russia choose to join the Allies? Well Russia had some friends in the Allies' group, like France and Britain. These friends talked to Russia and asked for help in the war. Just like when your friends ask you to play together, Russia chose to support its friends.

Furthermore, Germany in the other group, the Central Powers, was not so friendly with Russia. They had already had many disagreements and power struggles. Russia also wanted to help its friend Serbia, which was being bullied by another country called Austria-Hungary. They too were a part of the Central Powers working with Germany. In addition Russia wanted to gain more land. They thought being in the war on the Allies side could help them gain more land.

Russia's entry into the war had a significant impact on the dynamics of the Eastern front. They were able to launch massive offensives on multiple fronts, pressuring the Central

Powers including Germany, Austria-Hungary and the Ottoman Empire. The sheer scale of the Eastern Front made it difficult for the Central Powers to mount a successful defence. Their battles along the Eastern Front included many major ones that shaped its course in history. Here are some of the most famous ones.

Battle of Tannenberg

In the early days of World War I the Battle of Tannenberg was a crucial moment on the Eastern front. The German army under the brilliant leadership of General Paul Von Hindenburg and his chief staff, General Erich Ludendorff made strategic moves that would echo throughout history.

In the early stages of the war the Russian Empire launched an offensive into East Prussia, a region that was then part of Germany. The Russians planned to quickly advance into German territory, however General Hindenburg along with Ludendorff executed a masterful strategy. Imagine them orchestrating the defence like skilled conductors leading an orchestra.

The German forces lured the Russians into a trap near Tannenberg which is present day Poland. It was kind of like setting a snare for a huge bear to walk into. Here the German army surrounded the Russian forces isolating them from reinforcements and supply lines. Thousands of Russian soldiers were taken prisoner and their advance into East Prussia was halted which resulted in a decisive victory for the Germans. (Jordan & Neiberg, 2014)

Gorlice-Tarnów Offensive

In 1915, German and Austro-Hungarian forces launched a massive assault on the Eastern Front, focusing their efforts on the Gorlice-Tarnów region in present-day Poland. This was an impressive comeback in a tense situation. After a period of quiet, it suddenly became as intense as a thunderstorm. Gas warfare was one of the Central Powers' terrible new strategies that helped them breach the Russian lines. The Russians were forced to withdraw due to this offensive, which marked a decisive shift in the balance of power on the Eastern Front. Overall, this offensive had a major impact, shifting the balance of power and increasing the intensity of the conflict on the Eastern Front. (DiNardo, 2010)

The Brusilov Offensive

Now fast forward to 1916 and imagine a massive storm that was gathering on the Eastern Front. Russia under the command of General Alexei Brusilov launched a massive and well-planned assault against the Central Powers. This was like a thunderous roar that shook the foundations of the Austria-Hungarian empire.

Brusilov's mission was supposed to be a distraction, but it cost the Russian army dearly. In order to break through the enemy lines, Brusilov had smaller groups of Russian soldiers attack the enemy's weaknesses. This was unlike the typical military tactic of the time, which involved sending large numbers of troops in one go. On the Western Front, generals from France, Germany, and Britain all used similar tactics. They employed these strategies at a battle known as Verdun. In subsequent times, the Germans made extensive use of them, with excellent results.

Ultimately the Brusilov Offensive is remembered as one of the deadliest battles in history. Sadly, many people got hurt in this mission. Russia suffered almost a million casualties. Austria-Hungary and Germany also had many casualties, again nearly a million. Looking back, it's clear that Russia did well in this mission but ultimately failed to keep up its momentum. The Russian people got discouraged and stopped believing their leaders could win the war. Hard times had begun for the Russian Empire. The population was sick of the war and their leaders and demanded a change in government. The road now led to the tail end of World War 1 and the turbulence of the Russian Revolution. (Dowling, 2008)

The Russian Revolution

In 1917 Russia was beginning to go through major changes. It felt like pieces of a huge puzzle were being taken apart and put back together in completely new arrangements. The Russian Revolution was a massive event that was about to have consequences across the vast expenses of the Russian Empire. In fact it would be felt all the way across the landscape of World War 1.

Whilst World War 1 was still going on, something very important happened in Russia. In February 1917, there was a revolution in Russia called the "February Revolution." People were so fed up with the way their country was being run that they decided they no longer wanted a monarchy. Just like in a fairy tale when an evil king or queen is deposed, they ordered the royal couple to leave the country.

In October 1917 another exciting thing happened, called the "October Revolution." The government was overthrown at this time by a group headed by Vladimir Lenin. Bolsheviks was the name given to them. To all appearances, they had a new strategy for leading the nation. Meanwhile with the rest of the world caught up in World War 1, Russia underwent all of these transformations. Not only was there a major war, but Russia was also undergoing significant changes and adventures of its own. You couldn't have picked a more significant era in history! (Riasanovsky & Watson, 1991)

Now the changes weren't limited to just politics. Changes

extended deep into society, culture and even the fabric of everyday life. The old ways of life and hierarchies were challenged with a new era that was dawning. Imagine it like a massive wave sweeping out the old ways and bringing in the new. This was a period of both excitement and uncertainty where people were faced with massive changes happening around them on a daily basis. This chapter of revolution and change in Russia was an important moment not only in the country's history but also the outcomes of World War 1. A new era was unfolding as the world watched with anticipation to see how these changes would impact the war's final stages.

For the soldiers fighting on the Eastern fronts the changes had direct consequences. The Russian army which was once a powerful force was now in chaos. Soldiers were leaving the front lines to join the revolutionaries back home. Discipline had fallen off as had the ability to mount effective offensives. The Central Powers notably Germany saw this as an opportunity. With Russia consumed by the revolution, the Central Powers shifted their forces to the Western Front in a bid for a decisive victory there. On the grand chessboard one side had suddenly withdrawn some of their pieces which now created opportunities for their opponent on the board. (McMeekin, 2017)

Lenin's Bold Move

Vladimir Lenin and the Bolshevik Party had a new vision for Russia after seizing power in the city of Petrograd. It was like a magic trick, except instead of producing a rabbit from a hat, their goal was to get Russia out of World War 1.

Lenin and his team were well aware of the devastating effects the war was having on Russia and its people. So, they came up with a revolutionary plan. They signed the "Treaty of Brest-Litovsk" with the Central Powers (Germany and

Austria-Hungary) in March of 1918. This was a really daring step! When they signed this treaty, it officially meant that Russia was no longer part of World War 1. It was like saying, "We're done with this war." And as the ink dried on that agreement, something amazing happened on the map of the war. The fighting on the Eastern Front, where Russia was, stopped too. (Magnes, 1919)

When Russia left the war it created a dominant effect on the Eastern front. The Central Powers could now shift their forces to the Western Front where they sought a decisive victory. The withdrawal of Russia also created opportunities for new nations that emerged in its wake such as Ukraine and the Baltic States to become more independent. These changes continue to have impacts up to the present day.

With the Russian Revolution withdrawal we now move into the final years of World War 1. The conflict was still raging and as we embark on the final leg of our journey we'll explore how old it developed and ultimately concluded. So dear time travellers, fasten your seatbelts as we journey through the turbulent final years of World War 1.

Vladimir Lenin speaking to a Russian crowd

PART 3:
FINAL YEARS

CHAPTER 10
AMERICA JOINS THE FIGHT

• • • • • • • • • •

As we enter the final years of World War 1, you will witness history that was about to take a massive turn. New alliances were forming and the global landscape would be changed forever. Just when everyone thought they'd seen it all, a new player entered onto the war's grand stage. The United States of America was that player. Their entry changed the tide of the war and the course of history forevermore.

In the early 20th century the United States was a growing nation, full of power and potential. Imagine it like a giant eagle that was ready to spend its wings. In those early days of World War 1 they watched from the sidelines. Until then they had decided to remain neutral but as events in Europe unfolded, they could no longer stay on the sidelines.

In this chapter we will explore the United States' involvement in World War 1. We'll delve into the background of their entry, the heated debates it sparked in the United

States and the effect it had on the war's path. In this story, a country finds its voice on the international stage with consequences that ripple far beyond its borders.

The United States in the Early 20th Century

At the start of the 20th century the United States was going through a massive transformation. Its economy was booming and it was on track to become an industrial powerhouse. Factories churned out goods and the country contained vast resources. From the Atlantic to the Pacific, the United States was a vast country with a rapidly expanding population.

When World War 1 broke out in Europe, the United States first took a policy of remaining neutral. During his second term in office, President Woodrow Wilson stood by his earlier decision to keep the United States out of the war. Many Americans still had vivid memories of the destruction caused by the earlier Civil War in their country. Rightly so they were nervous to get involved in yet another war, especially one on faraway shores.

Submarines and secret messages

Germany's naval tactics were a major factor that put America's neutrality to the test. German U-boats were responsible for the loss of many Allied and American merchant ships. In a major event, the RMS Lusitania, a British ocean liner, was sunk by a German U-boat off the coast of Ireland in May of 1915. Several hundred Americans were amongst over a thousand passengers who died. Tensions between the United States and Germany escalated as a result of this shocking event.

Adding to the tension British intelligence had intercepted and decoded what became known as "the Zimmerman Telegram" in early 1917. In this secret message, Germany was asking Mexico if they wanted to team up against the United States if the United States joined the fight against Germany. It was like if two kids were fighting and one of them asked another kid to help them against the third kid. (Tuchman, 2014)

So, these two things, the sinking of the Lusitania and the discovery of the secret message, made people in the United States very angry at Germany. They saw Germany as the bad guys. Newspapers and posters talked a lot about how bad Germany was which made more people in the United States think that maybe they shouldn't stay neutral. In simple terms, finding out about the secret message and the sinking of the Lusitania made people in the United States change their minds about staying out of the argument. They started thinking maybe they should help the other countries who were not friends with Germany. (O'Sullivan, 2014)

President Wilson's dedication to a diplomatic solution continued despite the escalating tensions. He attempted to negotiate an end to the fighting. However, German U-boats kept attacking ships from the United States and its allies. In addition, after the Zimmerman Telegram was made public, President Wilson finally addressed Congress. In his request for a declaration of war against Germany on April 2, 1917, he cited the need to protect democracies and ensure global peace. After the declaration was approved by Congress, the United States officially entered World War 1 on the side of The Allies. (Seymour, 1921)

Following on, The United States quickly increased its military forces. To meet the demands of World War I, their armed forces needed to be expanded and modernised. The draft was legalised by the Selective Service Act of 1917, which enlisted millions of young American men. Factories joined the race producing weapons, equipment and supplies for the US military. The US had already been an effective supplier to the Allies providing them with much needed resources. Now they compounded on that with their own supplies. (States, 1918)

American soldiers began arriving on the Western Front in France. Their arrival strengthened the Allied Forces providing the troops with fresh power and enthusiasm. The American soldiers were eager to contribute to the war efforts and their presence boosted the morale of the tired and war fatigued Allies. With the American presence the balance of power was beginning to shift in favour of The Allies. American troops, resources and financial support greatly strengthened the Allied War efforts. The Central Powers were now faced with the combined might of The Allies and fresh American forces. Now they would find it very difficult to keep up.

World War 1 was still raging on and it was like a really big game with many countries involved. At this point, the United States was becoming super strong and important. In the global landscape they were becoming one of the leaders of the whole game. Ultimately they would have a big say in what happened next. Overall it was like the start of a time when the United States would become a really big and powerful country in the world.

Now it's time for us to go back in time a little. We're fastly turning the pages of history and we've reached an important moment during World War 1 called the "Nivelle Offensive." This was a really brave plan to break the stalemate. Simply this means when two sides cannot move forward as was the case in this time of the war. It was like trying to unblock a big traffic jam. Come along with us as we learn more about this big event and how it made a huge difference in the history of World War 1.

President Woodrow Wilson addressing Congress

CHAPTER 11
HIGH-STAKES ON THE WESTERN FRONT

Now let's step back into the pages of World War 1 history and explore a critical moment known as The Nivelle Offensive. This was a high stakes game of war where each side believed they had the winning strategy. It was a grand plan to break the stalemate on the Western Front. So as we dive deep into the history of World War 1 let us unravel the threads of this daring strategy and the world changing events that followed.

The Nivelle Offensive took place in April to May of 1917. It was a major military operation led by General Robert Nivelle of the French Army against the German forces on the Western Front in France. General Robert Nivelle was like the coach of a sports team but instead of sports games he was in charge of armies. In the game of war his plan was to help his team the Allies to defeat the Central Powers.

The general's plan for his troops was ambitious. He

planned to throw off the other team's defences in a bid to help his side win the war. Part of his plan was to launch a massive assault on the enemy, reclaim the territory they had lost and restore peace in the area. In April of 1917, he led a massive French offensive. Much like scoring the first goal of a soccer match, his team made significant early progress, gaining ground and experiencing initial success.

The Germans however were strong opponents. With solid defences they protected their own net like a locked fortress. When neither side could break the other's defences, the battle dried out into a stalemate not unlike a goalless draw in a soccer match. For a long time neither side could make any kind of progress.

The French soldiers faced a challenging situation which caused low morale and a lack of teamwork. Problems like not getting enough to eat and having poor equipment only added to this. Many troops were discouraged and didn't want to play the game of war any longer. It upset and frustrated them a lot.

Ultimately General Nivelles strategy hadn't unfolded as he planned. There was no declaration of victory or the longed-for peace on the battlefield. To use a sports analogy, it was like the team had put in countless hours of practice for a championship game, but when the big moment finally came, everything went wrong. Far from the goal, there was no sign of winning yet.

The French soldiers had moved forward and gained a lot of ground but they had run into something very tough called the Hindenburg line. This was like a super strong wall the Germans had built and it stopped the French soldiers in their tracks. But the French leader General Nivelle didn't want to give up. Even though many of his soldiers were getting hurt, he kept ordering them to charge headfirst into the enemy. By

April 25th, a great deal of sadness had been brought on by the loss of many French soldiers.

Meanwhile, in a town called Arras, British troops were engaged in fierce fighting. They had done well with the help of Canadian troops. Together they had made good progress. The conquest of the lofty hill of Vimy Ridge inspired national pride. However, things were becoming extremely difficult for the French. Because they were exhausted and no longer believed their leaders, many soldiers refused to go into battle. There were mutinies as a result, in which soldiers refused to carry out orders. Many of the troops were dissatisfied because they felt they had been overworked and wanted to return home to be with their families. (Cave & Sheldon, 2007)

Eventually General Pétain succeeded General Nivelle as the nation's leader. He showed more compassion and understanding toward the troops, sparing them harsh punishment. It was common practice to execute or imprison those found guilty of mutiny. Some were spared by Pétain's leadership. It took a long time, however, for the soldiers to begin to trust their leaders again. General Pétain was charismatic and rallied his troops back on their feet. Players adapted their strategies based on what they had learned from previous encounters. Everyone learned from their past mistakes and gained an appreciation for the difficulty and complexity of war.

The Nivelle Offensive with its grand plan and determined efforts left a lasting impact on the course of World War 1. However as history often shows us even the most ambitious strategies can face significant challenges. In the aftermath of this intense chapter of war several crucial lessons had been learned. The Allies had learned to adapt and understood that leadership just like in sports when a coach isn't achieving the results it might be time to make a change. General Nivelle's replacement by General Pétain showed the importance of having leaders who could not only plan big but also respond effectively to evolving circumstances.

Ultimately The Nivelle Offensive served as a reminder of how complicated and challenging war could be. Moving forward strategies and future battles would have to be adaptable. Just like Charles Darwin's theory of evolution says that "It is not the strongest of the species that survives, nor the most intelligent that survives. It is the one that is most adaptable to change." This is a lesson that goes beyond war and games but it can also be applied to our own lives. Being adaptable and flexible in your approach can be crucial for success. (Darwin, n.d.)

With new leadership, improved strategies and a more united front, the Allies slowly started to gain the upper hand in the war. This was like the soccer team coming from behind to tie the game and then take the lead. Over time, these changes led to a series of successful offensives by the Allies. The war had begun to turn in their favour.

Now as we turn the page, we're stepping into the exciting final stages of the war, where incredible adventures and important moments are just around the corner. Get ready to witness some truly historic moments as we dive into the daring Sinai and Palestine Adventure. (Murphy, 2015)

French soldiers on a battlefield in World War 1

CHAPTER 12
THE SINAI AND PALESTINE ADVENTURE

Building on what we've learned from the Nivelle Offensive we now move forward onto the next thrilling chapter of our journey through the history of World War 1. We've travelled across many battlefields, explored strategies and covered stories that have shaped the course of the war. Now let's venture out into desert sands and ancient lands as we dive into the captivating Sinai and Palestine campaigns of 1917 to 1918 towards the end of the war.

Imagine a vast and seemingly endless landscape where history meets the horizon. In this chapter we begin an adventure that takes us through the shifting stands at the Sinai Peninsula and the historic lands of Palestine. Here you'll discover a tale of daring manoeuvres and cultural encounters in a fight for control over key territories. Saddle up on your camel and get ready!

As we dive into this fascinating chapter of World War 1

history we will explore the aims and challenges faced by the forces involved in this campaign. We will witness the epic battles and high-level strategies that unfolded against the backdrop of the desert. From the legendary figures who led these campaigns to the brave soldiers who endured the harsh conditions their stories will be brought back to life.

But that's not all! We'll also explore the impact of the Sinai and Palestine campaigns on the wider landscape of World War 1. Just like the sands of the desert shift with time, so too did the balance of power during this campaign and that ultimately shaped the future of these lands. So prepare yourselves and get ready to journey into the scorching sands of the Sinai and the ancient paths of Palestine.

Strategies and goals

We begin the story by outlining the aims of this campaign which were like pieces of a giant puzzle. The Allies had several strategic goals. Firstly they wanted control of the Suez canal which was like a busy highway but instead of cars there were ships. The Suez Canal was a crucial part of the British Empire that provided a direct route to its colonies in Asia and india. Therefore they wanted to protect and control this lifeline.

Next they wanted to disrupt the Ottoman Empire which was Allied with Germany. The Ottoman Empire was a powerful force in the middle east. The campaign was aimed to weaken the Ottomans, disrupt their empire and eventually push them out of the region. Furthermore, opening up a new front would distract their opponent from their efforts in Europe.

The British were led by General Edmund Allenby. On the other side the Ottoman Empire received support from German advisors and troops to defend the region. There they had built up a strong line of defence and were determined to hold their ground. (Allenby, 2004)

Battle of Beersheba (October 1917)

Welcome to an important moment in the Sinai and Palestine campaign, the Battle of Beersheba. This was like a high stakes chess game taking place on the desert sands. Beersheba was an oasis found in a vast and scorching desert landscape. Inside of it was a precious resource that both sides needed, water. Within this oasis there were many wells that could quench the thirst of troops and horses.

General Sir Edmund Allenby, one of Britain's most successful commanders during World War 1 had come up with a daring plan. He understood that by taking over Beersheba it would be vital for the campaign's success. However the town was already heavily defended by Ottoman and German forces. The Australian light horse cavalry would be the answer to swiftly move in and evade the defences. Led by General Harry Chauve they were a close ally of the British forces. Like knights in an epic battle they mounted their horses with bravery and charged towards Beersheba. The space between them and Beersheba was vast and exposed them to enemy fire. Reaching Beersheba would require speed and valour.

On October 31 1917 at sunset, the Australian Light Horse cavalry launched a daring challenge. Kicking up clouds of dust they raced across the desert towards Beersheba. The Ottoman defenders watched with shock and disbelief as the cavalry charged towards them. It was a thrilling race to capture the town's wells! As they closed in on Beersheba they faced deadly machine gun fire and artillery. The odds were clearly stacked against them but with determination like knights on a quest they raced on and prepared for close combat.

As they approached Beersheba the Ottoman soldiers tried

to hold them back but the mighty cavalry smashed through like a powerful wave crashing against the shores. Successfully they captured Beersheba and in doing so they secured precious water sources. It was like finding a hidden treasure deep within the desert. The success relieved the urgent need for water and allowed the Allies to continue their advances into the desert. This was a significant turning point in the Sinai and Palestine Campaign. The Allies together with the Australian Light Horse cavalry had played a crucial role in the war efforts. Triumph and valour had won amidst the challenging desserts. (Daley, 2009)

The capture of Jerusalem

Imagine a long time ago, there was a big, important city called Jerusalem. Many people believed it was a very special place because it held a lot of meaning for their religion and culture. At that time it was ruled by a powerful group called the Ottoman Empire who were like the bosses of that area. But some other countries, like Britain, wanted to free Jerusalem from the rule of the Ottoman Empire. They believed that Jerusalem should be in the hands of the people who lived there and not some faraway empire.

In December 1917, British soldiers, led by the brave general, Sir Edmund Allenby, came to take back Jerusalem from those other rulers. This was a really big deal because it meant that Jerusalem would no longer be under their control. General Allenby had a plan and it was not just about winning a war but also about being really careful not to harm the city. He wanted to make sure that the city was treated with respect, even during a time of war.

The battle to capture Jerusalem was a mix of using strong soldiers and negotiating with the people who were in charge of the city. Those rulers didn't want to give up Jerusalem easily, but eventually they had to leave. On December 9th, 1917, the British soldiers entered the city. When they entered Jerusalem, General Allenby did something very special. He got down off his horse as a sign of respect for the city because it was considered holy by many. This moment was huge because it ended many, many years of the city being ruled by others and it started a new chapter in its history. The British soldiers came in with care and respect.

Even though capturing Jerusalem was a big deal, it also made people wonder what would happen next. It brought hope and change to the city, but it also raised questions about its future. Now anything that happened there would continue to affect the history of the region for a long, long time. (Allenby, 2004) (Grainger & Grainger, 2006)

The front line extends

In the early months of 1918, something important happened during World War 1. Imagine a big game of tug-of-war between two teams. The two opposing teams were the British Empire, representing the Allies and the Ottoman Empire, representing the Central Powers. The control of the Jordan Valley and its surrounding areas was a strategically important objective for both sides. This held key geographic and logistical significance in the broader context of the war in the Middle East.

In March and April of 1918, the British launched two big attacks known as the "First Transjordan" and the "Second Transjordan." These were like surprise moves in a chess game. The goal was for the British Empire to make sure they had control of the Jordan Valley. (Vatikiotis, 2017)

The British Empire soldiers moved through the sandy deserts, crossed rivers and even climbed mountains to reach the Jordan Valley. It was a bit like an adventurous journey.

When they got there, they set up their tents and waved their flags, saying, "This land is ours now!"

This was an important move in the war because it helped the British Empire control a vital part of the world map. It was a bit like capturing a key piece in a board game. The Jordan Valley was a gateway to other places and having it meant they held more power in the war.

Furthermore The British now had control of the Suez Canal and would continue to use it as vital supply routes for its Allies. The campaign along with many other factors contributed to the eventual downfall of the Ottoman empire like a chess player losing all their pieces one by one.

In conclusion the Sinai and Palestine campaigns were a chapter of World War 1 filled with strategic aims, bravery, battles and culture. All together it diverted Ottoman forces from many other fronts like a magician's trick distracting attention away from the main act. Ultimately this left a lasting impact on the Middle East and played a significant role in the course of World War 1 History.

The Australian Light Horse cavalry
racing across the dessert

CHAPTER 13
THE ALLIES MAKE THEIR FINAL PUSH FOR VICTORY

Welcome back time travellers! Now we're about to move from the deserts of the Sinai and Palestine campaigns into a new chapter filled with twists and turns. World War 1 was a long and tough war just as you've witnessed in the campaigns so far. At this point both sides had endured many hardships and the war had gone on far longer than anyone could have imagined. But just as the seasons change, so too does the course of war. As the war entered its final phases, the year 1918 witnessed a dramatic and important event known as the German Spring Offensive.

The German Spring Offensive

The German Spring Offensive, also called the Kaiserschlacht or "Kaiser's Battle" was a bold and risky move by the Central Powers, led by Germany, to break the stalemate on the Western Front. By early 1918 World War 1 had been raging on for almost four years. The Central Powers namely Germany and its allies were growing more desperate. Before the United States could fully launch its troops and resources, they planned to launch a massive offensive on the Western Front. Germany understood that the full involvement of the United States in the war would dramatically shift the odds in favour of their enemies. Therefore they wanted a head start.

On March 21 1918 the German Spring Offensive commenced. It began with a massive artillery barrage along the Western Front. This initial bombardment was followed by a strong German advance which used infiltration tactics to bypass strong points and gain ground quickly. The Germans were making bold moves in a bid to win big. Just like in a soccer game when one team scores early on it gives them a significant advantage. The Germans early scoring where they captured important towns and territory gave them significant momentum. Meanwhile on the other side, the Allies became nervous just like when your team is losing you would also become worried.

But big moves take up a lot of energy. The German players were starting to feel very tired. Supplies were running low and their soldiers were beginning to feel exhausted. Furthermore they had lost many teammates along the way. Losing members of your team is like losing players in a game, it hurts your chances of winning. Soon enough The United States' entry into the war also provided a morale boost to the Allies. More and more Americans were joining the game, giving the Allies a fresh boost of new enthusiasm.

A turning point occurred in July of 1918 when the Germans were attempting a daring offensive in the area around the Marne River. They wanted to capture Paris like it was a prize in a game. But the French team with support from The Americans refused them. Together they defended with determination in what became known as the Second Battle of

Marne. It marked a crucial turning point in the war. Here the French and American Coalition didn't just stop the German advance but they also pushed them backwards.

The German squad started to lose their early advantage. No longer were they moving forward along the field, but now they were retreating. They were overextended and running in many directions at once. The German Spring Offensive lost steam as a result of this shift in force. In the end, it was a wake-up call for the German players because it didn't go as they'd hoped.

The German Spring Offensive left the Central Powers with many unanswered questions. They began to question whether or not they had what it took to defeat their enemy, who now included the United States as one of many much larger players. Were they able to keep up?

As the war entered a new phase, the world watched in anticipation. In the next section we will explore the thrilling events that took place during this pivotal period. The Allies, fueled by determination and newfound strength, embarked on a remarkable campaign that would ultimately tip the scales in their favour. (Grehan & Mace, 2014)

The Hundred Days Offensive

The "Hundred Days Offensive" would prove to be a turning point in the outcome of World War 1, which was drawing to a close. It was like the fourth quarter of a nail-biting sporting event, when everything was on the line. In 1918 The Allies including the United Kingdom, France and now the United States were determined to bring the war to a victorious end. The Hundred Days Offensive was a series of offences launched by the Allies on the Western Front. Imagine it as a grand game with the Allies pushing back the Central Powers.

General Ferdinand Foch was the head coach of The Allies. But he was no ordinary coach. He was a master strategist drawing up masterful plans to guide the Allied Forces to victory. Imagine him as a conductor leading an orchestra to play together in a symphony. Under his command soldiers were ready to step forwards onto any field and give their best performance. Each soldier had their own unique strengths and skills. Some were star players famous for their bravery and leadership whilst others worked tirelessly behind the scenes.

The soldiers came from diverse backgrounds wearing different uniforms and speaking different languages. But they all shared the common goal, to bring an end to the war and emerge victorious. Together they trained hard, studied their enemies and followed their commanders orders. General Foch knew that to win this game he would have to coordinate the efforts of his diverse forces. This was a huge task to make sure that the efforts were in alignment and that everyone played their part. Carefully he planned and communicated with all the commanders to ensure the correct decisions were made on the pathway towards victory. With determination and bravery the soldiers followed their orders and faced the challenges head on. Together they charged forward, gaining ground, defending their positions and supporting their teammates. Together they endured many great hardships but together they showed courage and never gave up no matter how tough things became.

In September 1918 the Allies gathered their best forces and launched a massive attack known as The Battle of Saint-Mihiel. It was a daring battle where soldiers climbed over castle walls in a determined effort to breach the seemingly impossible Hindenburg line. Brave soldiers advanced into enemy terrain like valiant knights in shining armour. They were faced with fierce opposition but their resolve was unbreakable. As artillery thundered like the roar of dragons they pressed forwards inch by inch to victory.

The Battle of Saint-Mihiel was a game changer that showcased the Allies strength, strategy and unwavering spirit. The Hindenburg line, as mighty as it seemed, ultimately was not invincible. The fortress now showed cracks and the walls had been breached which sent shock waves through enemy lines. The mighty German defences had been pierced and the game of war was now tilting in favour of the Allies.

Like tales of valiant knights and castles, The Battle of Saint-Mihiel was an heroic chapter in the story of World War 1. The lessons learned showed us that with determination and teamwork we can overcome the greatest of challenges. For what was once thought to be invincible had now been breached and victory was now within reach of The Allies.

As the Hundred Days Offensive continued, the Central Powers faced even more challenges. Their armies were getting more tired as they struggled with the relentless attacks. Just like in the game of chess when your opponent's king is cornered, the Allies had pushed the Central Powers into a corner. As they were backed into the corner the Central Powers began to surrender. Bulgaria was the first to give up followed by the Ottoman Empire and then Austria-Hungary. Each surrender was like a player leaving the game, one by one with each surrender weakening the Central Powers.

Germany soon realised that they were hopeless, alone and faced a turning point. After a change of government in Germany, the two sides agreed to an armistice. To use a sports comparison, this was like requesting a timeout. The end of World War 1 was marked by the end of fighting on November 11, 1918.

The Hundred Days offensive was a remarkable chapter in the history of World War 1. In the darkest moments of conflict it showed that with determination and teamwork victory could be found. This was a testament to the enduring human spirit. Ultimately the impact of The Hundred Days offensive went far beyond the battlefield. In Europe its echoes were felt across the lands, bringing an end to old empires and giving birth to new nations. The world was changing and the legacy of these momentous days remind us of vital lessons. Unity and cooperation in our quest for peace and a brighter future is essential.

Now as we enter into the next part of our journey we will explore what happened in the aftermath of World War 1. We'll learn about the peace deals that sought to heal the scars of conflict and the new world that emerged from the ashes. This is a tale of hope, diplomacy and a pursuit for lasting peace. So dear young historians let us now turn the page and discover the final chapters of this epic story. (Langley, 2009)

American soldiers arriving on the battlefields

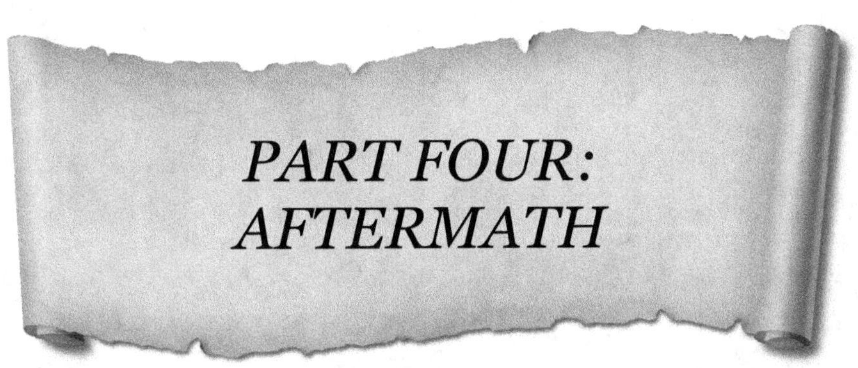
PART FOUR:
AFTERMATH

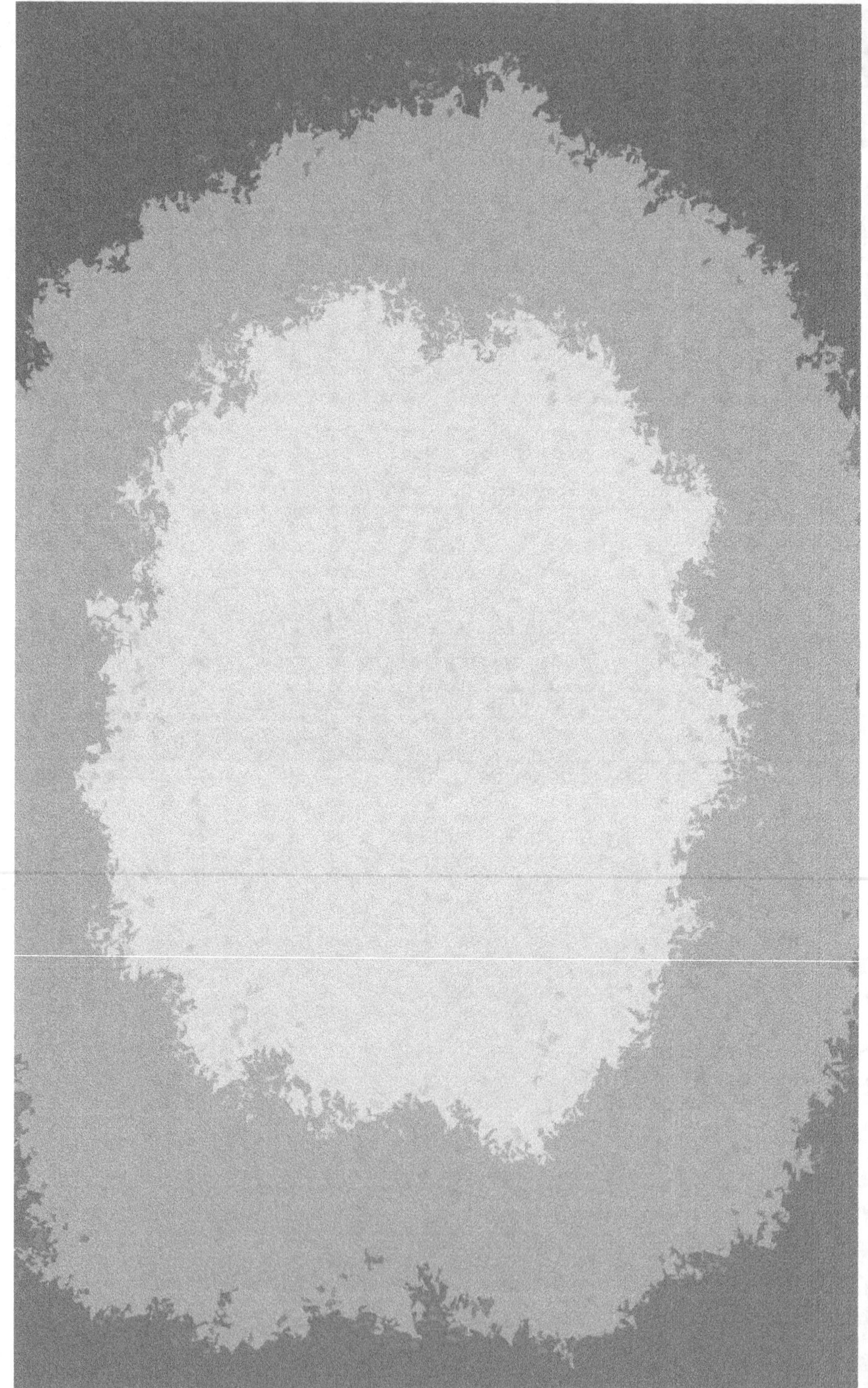

CHAPTER 14
PEACE AT LAST

• • • ● • ● ● • ● • ● • • ●

After many long years of conflict and countless sacrifices the world was finally ready for a new chapter. When the guns fell silent on November 11th 1918, World War 1 had officially ended. This was a momentous occasion filled with relief and hope as nations came together to seek a lasting peace. In this chapter and in this final section of the book we're about to embark on the final leg of our journey through World War 1. Here will learn about the formal end of the war and the peace deals that took place to heal the wounds of the past. But would peace last?

Armistice Agreements

Imagine a big game of hide and seek where everyone was tired of hiding. World War 1 ended more or less like this. Armistice agreements were signed by a number of countries to end hostilities. On November 11th, 1918, the most famous treaty was signed with Germany. When the fighting finally stopped, leaders from many countries packed their bags and travelled to the city of Paris. Here they arranged a big meeting called the Paris Peace Conference. Imagine this like a meeting of superheroes who wanted to make the world a better place in the aftermath of World War 1. (Wiest, 2014)

Various world leaders descended upon this historic city for a meeting that would shape the future. In attendance there was President Woodrow Wilson, the wise and thoughtful leader of the United States. Georges Clemenceau, the determined and fierce French leader. David Lloyd George, the clever and cautious leader from the United Kingdom. And last but not least, Vittorio Orlando, the Italian leader who brought his nation's aspirations to the table.

During the Paris peace conference the League of Nations was created with the goal of maintaining peace in the world. Imagine a club where countries could talk about problems instead of fighting. This is what the League of Nations was like. However not every country was invited to join the club and this made things a little bit tricky.

The Treaty of Versailles

Now let's learn about a very important document that was drafted in those days. In June of 1919, the Allies handed Germany a rulebook in the form of the Treaty of Versailles. This was similar to a teacher giving a misbehaving student a list of rules to follow. The Paris Peace Conference set out to make the world a better place.The Treaty of Versailles was its lasting legacy, leaving behind renewed optimism for a peaceful future.

The Treaty of Versailles had some tough terms for Germany. They would have to give up land which they once called their own. Furthermore they would have to reduce their military to a fraction of its former size, like a giant becoming a mouse. Lastly and if that wasn't enough, they were told to pay large sums of money to the countries that had been hurt during the war.

Chaos and uncertainty filled the air during this time as people around the world tried to pick up the pieces after the war. The Treaty of Versailles was widely criticised for being too harsh on Germany. They had to give up land, reduce their military, and make major financial payments to other nations. Financially and emotionally, Germany was put in a tough spot. Sadness and frustration plagued the community. There would be unintended consequences.

But the Paris Peace Conference wasn't just about Germany. Leaders made treaties with other countries too. Austria-Hungary, Bulgaria and the Ottoman Empire also had to sign treaties. Each treaty contained rules about land borders and what these countries could and could not do. Imagine the maps of the world transforming before your very eyes like a magical atlas. This is kind of what happened at the end of World War 1.

The aftermath of war led to massive changes on the map of the world. It was like a reshuffling of countries and borders. Some countries vanished from the map all together like old puzzles with missing pieces. Meanwhile empires that had once ruled vast territories in the past like the Austria-Hungarian Empire and the Ottoman Empire crumbled into history. In their place new nations were born each with their own identity and aspirations.

Now it wasn't as easy as just scribbling new lines on paper to redo the maps. It was like putting together a massive puzzle where the pieces didn't always fit. Many issues came up. Citizens in Europe and the Middle East watched in amazement as their borders changed. Disputes and wars broke out when communities that had lived together for decades suddenly found themselves in different countries.

Redrawing the maps was a difficult task, but it was done in the name of peace. Just like any puzzle, it presented its own unique set of difficulties. The aftermath of which would be felt for many years to come. (Byers, 2017)

Consequences

World War 1 was a really, really big fight that happened all over the world. Many people got hurt and many lost their lives. The war didn't just hurt people's bodies, it also made their hearts very sad. When the brave soldiers came back home, many of them had been hurt. They had scars on their bodies from the fighting and when they got back to their houses, things were very different. It was like going away for a long time and coming back to find that your room has changed.

Families were really sad too. Many had lost someone they loved in the war and they missed them a lot. Imagine if someone you really cared about wasn't there anymore and you couldn't see or talk to them. It was a time when the whole world felt very different and everyone had to try to get used to these big changes.

World War 1 was a very sad time for a lot of people. But it's also a time when people learned the importance of peace and working together to make the world a better place, so that wars like this wouldn't happen again. People understood that talking and working together was a better solution than fighting without an end in sight. Peace was cherished and it must be protected. As the world leaders gathered in Paris and the ink dried on the signed agreements they hoped that lessons of the past would lead to a more peaceful future. But little did they know that the impacts of their decisions would lead to many more challenges in the years to come.

Rebuilding nations

In the devastating aftermath of World War 1, the world was faced with the challenging task of rebuilding nations. The world was scarred with wounds from the war. Many cities lay in ruins and hearts were filled with sadness. Close your eyes and for a moment imagine how the world was after World War 1. The aftermath was like when a mighty storm sweeps through a city leaving behind destruction and despair. Many countries had been torn apart by the conflict leaving their lands scarred.

Cities around the world had been reduced to rubble. Grand buildings and proud homes that once defined these communities were now just piles of debris and broken dreams. Streets that once echoed with the laughter of children and the joys of daily life were now silent like ghost towns. People were slowly emerging back to daily life as they faced the task of rebuilding their communities from the ground up. It was much like trying to reconstruct a giant jigsaw but many pieces were missing or damaged beyond repair.

From the devastation that had gripped the world for many years before emerged a remarkable spirit of resilience. This was the force that defied the despair that the war had witnessed. The world collectively decided to rise from the ruins and move past the hurt, pain and suffering they had endured. Communities found strength in unity and became pillars of support for each other. It was as if the world was starting to unite once again like a grand symphony where every instrument played a vital role contributing to the melody of recovery.

This spirit of resilience transcended borders and politics. Former enemies who had once faced each other on the battlefield now worked together with the goal of rebuilding the world. It was a global team effort with many nations sharing resources, knowledge and hope. Like a group of friends they worked together to mend the wounds.

As time passed the scars of war slowly began to fade. Cities that were once in ruins were reconstructed and the streets were bustling with life once more. Economies that had crumbled under the pressures of conflict began to recover. Industries were rebuilt and trade routes were reestablished. Nations having realised the severe consequences of war were now committed to a different path, a path of peace.

War wounds were both a warning and a reminder of what had happened in the past. The lessons that the world had learned from this long war were profound. Insights that would not be quickly forgotten. Nations were now more interested in diplomatic and collaborative approaches to conflict resolution. It was like starting over, a clean slate on which to build a future of harmony and cooperation, using the lessons learned from the past as a map. Now, let's examine how the major countries involved in the war dealt with the aftermath.

In France the scars of war ran deep within its soils. Many regions had been devastated by trench warfare and battles. Cities like Verdun and Ypres were significantly damaged but the French communities worked tirelessly to rebuild them. France also played a key role in the post war negotiations with Paris hosting the venue for the signing of the Treaty of Versailles.

In Germany, one of the Central Powers faced significant challenges after the war. The Treaty of Versailles left them with severe consequences, restrictions and territorial losses. As a result major cities like Berlin and Munich saw political changes and struggled with a battered economy. The people there faced hard times and had to navigate the turbulent post war times.

In the United Kingdom, a major player of the Allies' efforts had drained its resources and spending. After the war the communities worked together to rebuild the British economy and infrastructure to become strong once again.

In Belgium parts of the country had been major battlegrounds during World War 1. Together these regions reconstructed back to its best. Their efforts stood as a symbol of resilience and remembrance.

In Eastern Europe, The Austro-Hungarian Empire fell apart after the war. This led to the establishment of separate nations, with Austria and Hungary becoming independent republics. The Treaty of Saint-Germain (for Austria) and the Treaty of Trianon (for Hungary) formalised these changes. Many other nations, including Czechoslovakia and Yugoslavia, emerged from the territories of the former empire. Serbia became a part of the Kingdom of Serbs, Croats and Slovenes, which was later renamed Yugoslavia in 1929. Other nations in the region such as Poland had been deeply affected by the war. Poland was restored as an independent nation after more than a century of division. Efforts were focused on rebuilding this nation's infrastructure and economy. (Powers & Martin, 1924)

In the United States their country didn't experience any physical devastation like the European cities, but it played a significant role in the post war reconstructions. American industry boomed once again as they provided aid and loans to other nations. They played a central role in facilitating international recovery and trade.

In Africa, nations called for independence in the post-war period. In the Middle East the Ottoman Empire was dismantled and new maps were redrawn. This led to the creation of new countries like Iraq, Turkey and Syria with consequences that are felt to this day.

Ultimately all of these regions and countries face significant challenges and opportunities in the aftermath of World War 1. Even though they carried the scars of war they also carried the promise of rebuilding and shaping a better future. Their resilience and determination of working together played a central part to this transformative period in history.

After the devastating events of World War 1, people all over the world wanted peace. There was a sigh of relief all around, but underlying tensions remained hot and ready to boil over at any moment. Come with us as we investigate the reasons why the search for lasting peace proved so difficult in the aftermath of this epic conflict.

Signing of The Treaty of Versailles in Paris

CHAPTER 15
A FRAGILE PEACE

As the dust settled after the chaos of World War 1 a desire for peace swept across the nations. It was like a sigh of relief that echoed around the globe. The Treaty of Versailles stood as a symbol of hope and peace. However beneath the surface tensions began to simmer like a pot of water on the verge of boiling over. In this chapter we explore the post-war world and reveal the fragility of peace.

In the aftermath of World War 1 the Treaty of Versailles was an important document aimed at shaping a new better future. But it wasn't perfect, it was like a puzzle with many pieces that didn't quite fit together and had many missing pieces. Imagine this grand jigsaw puzzle with each piece representing a different nation's interests. At the centre of the puzzle was Germany, a once powerful empire but was now defeated and humiliated. Part of the Treaty of Versailles presented Germany with a huge bill for all the damage and destruction that was caused during the war. Of course this was a huge burden for them to take on.

Without truly understanding the consequences the Treaty of Versailles ultimately left Germany humiliated and resentful. This once fierce and proud nation had been shamed and wounded like a cornered animal. Humiliation and resentment would simmer beneath the surface waiting for the right conditions to ignite. Many questioned whether the approach in terms of the treaty would really lead to lasting peace or whether it would lead to future conflicts. Many thought it was like a ticking time bomb with the potential to explode into renewed hostilities.

Understand that true and lasting peace often requires understanding, empathy and compromise. It's like trying to mend a broken friendship. If we just blame and make demands it will only make things worse. Instead we need to find common ground, listen to each other and work towards shared goals which are more effective in building a peaceful foundation.

Rise of Ideologies

In the aftermath of World War 1 major changes happened in the political landscape which gave rise to potent ideologies. But what exactly are ideologies?

- Democracy
  Imagine you and your friends want to choose a game to play. In a democracy everyone gets a say and the game that most people choose is the one you'll all play.

- Communism
  Imagine a big box of crayons that everyone shares. In communism, people work together and share things so that everyone has what they need. But sometimes people don't share and corruption makes things unfair.

- Capitalism

Imagine a lemonade stand you set up. You work hard, make lemonade, and sell it to people. In capitalism, you can earn money by selling things you make or provide.

- Socialism
  Imagine a class where everyone helps each other with homework. In socialism, the idea is that people work together to make sure everyone has what they need. For example, education and healthcare.

- Fascism
  Imagine a group where one person makes all the rules and everyone has to follow them without question. In fascism, one leader has total control and other people don't have much say.

- Anarchism
  Imagine a world where there are no teachers or parents and kids make all the rules themselves. In anarchism, there's no government or authority. People rely on cooperation instead of rules.

Remember, these are simple explanations and in the real world these ideologies are often more complex. People have different ideas about how they should work, but these descriptions should give you a basic understanding.

Now back to the aftermath of World War 1. In Russia communism led by leaders like Vladimir Lenin and the Bolsheviks was emerging as a new ideology. Their ideology was like a revolutionary force with the aim to create a society where wealth and power would be shared among the masses. Behind the scenes a group of determined individuals marched forwards into the uncharted territory. Their primary aim was to establish a classless society which was a grand new experiment to test whether such a vision could really become a reality. The Russian Revolution of 1917 began the first successful introduction of these ideas on a national scale. (Riasanovsky & Watson, 1991)

On the other side of the political spectrum fascism began to take root in Italy under the charismatic leadership of Benito Mussolini. This was a radical and authoritarian ideology that focused on consolidating power in a strong centralised state. Fascism spread like wildfire across Italy and beyond, igniting the flames of extreme nationalism and authoritarian rule. (Roberts, 2005)

Imagine these were two rivers of opposing currents, one represented communism with its calls for shared wealth and power whilst the other represented fascism with its calls for a powerful and centralised state. These ideologies clashed and competed for dominance. Ultimately they shaped the course of history in a turbulent post war period.

Post World War 1 the global landscape was a fertile ground for political ideologies and transformation. Clashes between communism and fascism would define the politics of the 20th century and lead to some consequential events.

The Great Depression

As our journey exploring the devastating post World War 1 era continues we are met with a sudden and devastating storm on the horizon, The Great depression. This was a global economic crisis that swept through the world in the aftermath of World War 1 leaving a trail of despair. The postwar world was a balancing act with nations trying to rebuild, recover and avoid further catastrophe.

The Great Depression was mostly caused by the drain on economies of World War 1. War is expensive and this one came at a great cost. The Great Depression was a chapter from history that showed us how deeply societies are connected with each other around the world. It also teaches us that with resilience, compassion and innovation we can find solutions even in times of adversity.

Imagine a world where families and communities were suddenly faced with collapsed economies. It was like their world had been turned upside down. Once they were rich and now they were poor with many losing their jobs, homes and savings in the blink of an eye. The Great Depression was like a huge monster lurking under the bed as a constant source of fear and uncertainty.

This economic catastrophe didn't affect just one nation, it affected the whole world. The world had been pushed into darkness where dreams of a better future had now turned into a nightmare. Nations were tested and their leaders faced massive challenges. Governments struggled to find solutions as their economics grappled with unprecedented challenges of unemployment, poverty and hunger. Families had to gather together to support each other but their resilience proved the human spirit to prevail even in the face of adversity. (McElvaine, 2010)

World War 2

In the 1920s nations worked hard to rebuild and hoped for a lasting peace. But many had deep wounds that were still felt deep within their nations. These wounds were far from healed and the memories of war still played out. In particular Germany felt the most hurt. As we learned earlier, The Treaty of Versailles had given them harsh penalties. It was like having all your favourite things taken from you and being told to sit in a cold room alone. Of course they were left feeling humiliated and resentful. As we learned from history, true peace comes from understanding and compromise rather than punishment. We must learn and listen. Now this had created tension in the nation and like a bomb ticking away its fuse was ready to ignite.

The world found itself in a delicate balance of peace. Dark storm clouds began to gather on the horizon which would cast long shadows over the entire world. In Germany there was a man called Adolf Hitler. He was quickly becoming famous through his captivating speeches that connected with the frustrations the nation faced in the aftermath of World War 1. Together with his group, the Nazis, they took over control of the country. People in Germany were fed up with the harsh conditions they had endured and with the fresh promises of Hitler and the Nazis, they believed their land would become powerful once again.

Germany grew back much stronger but they didn't stop there. They were hungry like a wolf. Adolf Hitler wanted to win back the territories they had lost in The Treaty of Versailles and to bring back together all the German speakers. He built up strong armies and was like a chess player ready to capture important pieces on the board. Swiftly he moved into other countries and in doing so he showed that he didn't care about the old agreements. This made people in Europe become worried as Germany's power grew. (Editors, 2017)

Meanwhile in Italy the charismatic leader Benito Mussolini and his fascist government wanted to make the government even more strong. His ideas spread quickly like wildfires, and threatened democracy and freedom. These two leaders were like villains who quickly rose with great power and didn't allow anyone to disagree with them. Whilst their countries grew stronger and their economies thrived they became greedy for more power. The world watched on as it became an uncertain place and the peace that had been established after World War 1 became even more fragile.

On the other side of the world some important things also happened. Nations argued about who should control certain areas of the world like chess pieces on a game board. Japan wanted more land and so they took over a place called Manchuria in 1931. As a result tensions were caused in Asia.

The world watched on as these territories and disputes gained momentum. Diplomatic efforts weren't working. People wanted change and if it meant using force then so be it. The leaders of the world were now playing dangerous games with high stakes and the consequences could be very disastrous for all involved. Even though many try to avoid the conflict by making concessions, ultimately it didn't stop the growing tensions. The world became like a stack of dominoes falling one by one as each diplomatic effort collapsed bringing the world closer to a new war. Just like we learned in this book those dominoes can fall quickly and lead to mass devastation.

As we near the events of World War 2 we must remember that history is more than just a bunch of old stories. History contains the choices people made, the actions they took and the consequences of those actions. As we conclude this challenging time in history let us remember that we have the power to choose cooperation and peace instead of war. We're now at the end of our exploration of World War I and how it led into World War 2. Dear reader that is a subject for another book and you can learn all about that in our book:

World War 2 History For Kids: A Timeline of Fascinating Facts, Characters and Stories of Courage that Inspire & Educate

https://www.amazon.com/dp/B0C7QW6T66

Struggles in Germany after World War 1

CONCLUSION

Well young time travellers, we've finally reached the end of our epic journey! Through the pages of World War 1 history we've been on an adventure that was filled with captivating stories, metaphors and powerful lessons. We have journeyed across continents through trenches and into the heart of one of the most important chapters in human history. As we get ready to step back into the present moment let us reflect on what we've learned from our adventure so far.

History is more than just a bunch of stories or a collection of dates and facts. It's a living breathing story of the people who came before us. By understanding the past we can gain better insights into the present and work towards a better future. But to do that we must learn from the past. The lessons we learn from history are not meant to be forgotten but they are meant to guide us to a better future.

The history of World War 1 was a dark and challenging chapter in history. Many brave soldiers lost their lives. Furthermore many women and children bravely supported efforts at home and on the battlefields. Their stories remind us that ordinary individuals can do extraordinary things and that even in the darkest of times there is always hope.

Close your eyes and imagine that you are a time traveller of today. Think of how the knowledge and insights you learn can help someone just like you in the future. Today you have the opportunity to promote peace, understanding and respect for others. Like a beacon of hope your actions can inspire others to make the world a better place. You too hold the keys to shape a better future.

Our modern world faces its own challenges and difficulties. But just like the brave soldiers, determined leaders and the homefront heroes of World War 1 you too can make a difference. Even though you are just one person, together with your collaboration you can make the world a better place. Even if it's the smallest of things such as taking responsibility for being a more kind and understanding human.

As our journey draws to an end the adventure doesn't have to stop here. History is a vast treasure trove that waits to be explored further. Imagine it as a book with never ending pages! Learning is never ending and there are countless stories and events to discover. Whether you're interested in other wars, ancient civilizations or the stories of heroes. Then you can learn more from our other books and videos which you can find on our website.

https://historybroughtalive.com/

Time travel may be the source of fiction or movies but we can also travel through time ourselves. In our own way we can jump back into history through the pages of a book. Keep the adventure alive in your hearts! Keep learning about history, together with your friends and family. Visit museums, read books and explore the wonders of the past. With each insight you'll gain a deeper understanding of the world and the diverse people who have shaped it. Each person, event and decision no matter how small has ultimately created the world that we know today. Whilst there were many tragic moments there have also been many triumphant ones which have paved the way of progress towards a better future.

Now it's time for you to think about how you can make the world a better place. What could you do to improve the world and go down in history? Maybe you could think up great inventions. Maybe you could help your community. Maybe you could be a better listener. Maybe you could work on being a more understanding person and help others.

Consider some of the projects that you could get involved in or the ways that you can cooperate with people from different backgrounds. Think of ways to protect our planet and its precious reverses. Maybe you could help others in need plant trees or stand up against injustice. Maybe you could volunteer in your community. Your actions even if they're small can ripple through time and create a positive impact for generations to come.

In our adventure we've stumbled across many hidden treasures and surprising moments from the past. Like opening a time capsule, history has revealed unexpected gems that have captivated our imaginations. You too can create your own time capsules. Gather items, write things down, take photos and savour important memories from your life. Most of all, be present to the moment and live it fully. In the future you'll look back on it with fondness as you'll be transported back to this moment in time to share your experience and insights with future generations.

As you grow older the stories and moments spent with

your elders will become even more precious. These are the most cherished things that will connect you to your family history and provide a deeper understanding of your roots. The stories of their lives, struggles and triumphs connect to your story. Close your eyes and imagine yourself old like your grandparents listening to their adventures and experiences. Reflect on those and begin making your own stories of greatness to pass down to future generations. Remember to help make our world a better place!

APPENDICE ONE
TIME TRAVELLER TOOL KIT

Before we say our final goodbyes we would like to celebrate your bravery! Just like the heroes of history, you have embarked on a discovery of learning from reading this book. As we gather here in the closing moments of our journey allow us to present you with the time traveller awards to strong explorers. These awards were created to celebrate your curiosity for knowledge and a determination to make history come alive. Now without further ado here are the awards!

- The Curiosity Award
  This goes to those who asked the most intriguing questions to explore into depths of the past.

- The Compassion Award
  This goes to those who were inspired by the stories of resilience and courage. For they showed empathy and kindness.

- The Time Travelling Award
  This goes to those who went the extra mile by reading and exploring further than beyond the pages of this book. Well done.

- The Future Shaper Award
  This goes to those who have been inspired to take action and make a positive impact on their communities. Congratulations.

Your journey through history doesn't have to end here. As we said before, history is a never-ending story. Many more time travelling methods are awaiting for you to explore. Here just a few of those:

Books

At History Brought Alive we offer many books from some of the most important chapters in history. We also recommend that you read from a diverse range of sources to transport to the different eras and introduce you to the fascinating times of the past. For more on us, please follow the link below.

https://historybroughtalive.com/

Movies

Allow the magic of the cinema to take you back to the past! Many movies have been made about various times in history from epic battles to personal stories of triumph and perseverance. Step back into time through the magic of movies.

Museums

Make plans to visit museums both near and far. These will take you back in time to history through the artefacts exhibits and experiences. Share the moments with your friends and families.

Remember once again that learning never ends. Continue to read, watch and explore. With each discovery you take a step towards becoming a better time traveller. As you carry the knowledge and lessons with you, consider sharing them with others. Just as you were inspired you have the power to ignite the inspiration with the next generation of history explorers.

Here are some ways to spark imaginations.

- History Themed Events & Gatherings
  Visit with friends and families to share stories and insights.

- History Clubs & Online Communities
  Meet with other time travellers to discuss your discoveries.

- Volunteering at Museums, Societies or Schools
  Share your love of history with others.

Keep inspiring others around you! Become a carrier of knowledge who passes on the magic of time travel to future generations. May your adventures continue and let the past guide you toward a brighter and more compassionate future.

Now as a final gift we have a "Time Travelers Tool Kit". This is like a magical collection of gifts and ideas allowing you to unleash your creativity and curiosity. Here you will find activities, ideas and projects that will take you back to the time of World War 1. Roll up your sleeves!

- The Mini Time Machine
  Building a time travelling machine might be a bit tricky! But we can use our own simple versions. Here is one example of how.

Grab an old shoe box and turn it into a mini time machine! Take some coloured paper and gather some tiny soldiers to recreate scenes from World War 1. As you look at this mini version of time it'll be like you're looking into a window of the past. Recreate those battlefields and moments from history

- Time Travel Journal
  Every time traveller needs a journal to record their adventures. Grab yourself a notebook or create a new one from scratch. Decorate it with a cardboard cover of World War 1 History. Make this your own history and fill it with your thoughts. Write down observations, lessons and ideas as you explore history.

- Historical Costumes
  Dive even deeper into the past by dressing up like the heroes of the past. Study the pictures of how people looked back in the days of World War 1. Create your own inspired outfits using simple sewing and crafting techniques. You can become a nurse, soldier or even a spy. Let their memories live on through you.

- Colouring Book
  Colouring is a fantastic way to dive into history. Most of the pictures from World War 1 are in black and white. Bring them back to life with colour, or create your own. Draw scenes from the war or famous images that capture the era. Share these with your friends and family to see if you can bring the history to life.

- Historical Maps
  Historical maps are another way to bring history to life. Explore maps from the past and add colour to highlight key areas and events. This will be like charting your own course through history.

These are just a few gateways to making history come alive! Remember there are endless other ways to immerse yourself in the past. Just grab your imagination and continue your adventures through history. Good luck on your journey!

APPENDICE TWO
TECHNOLOGY ADVANCEMENTS IN WORLD WAR 1

Imagine a world without smartphones, fast cars or planes soaring across the sky. Before World War 1 this is how the world was. People often travelled with horses and carriages. Meanwhile they wrote messages with pen and paper. But this era was the beginning of an incredible new world where new inventions and ideas were beginning to bloom. It was a time when people were dreaming of ways to make life better and easier. In this extra part of the book we'll journey back into time to explore this fascinating period when the world was swept up in the winds of change.

During World War 1 nations had to quickly develop and innovate to keep up with the challenges of the war. Many inventions and innovations emerged during this period. Here we will explore some of the major technological advancements in World War 1.

Weapons

Machine guns

Machine guns are powerful weapons that can fire many rounds of bullets in a short amount of time. These were placed on the front lines and in the trenches of World War 1. They were also mounted onto vehicles and planes ready to fire at enemies. Soldiers on the receiving end faced loud and devastating firepower. Overall they had a significant impact on the war's outcome making it more brutal and challenging for both sides.

Tanks

Tanks were invented as a response to the challenges of trench warfare in World War 1. British Engineers had first developed the tanks in secret and they were originally called land ships to keep the purpose hidden. Designed to navigate difficult terrain such as muddy trenches they were heavily armoured with machine guns and cannons. Tanks could steamroll through the enemy lines to create openings for soldiers. They were like fortresses rolling through enemy fire, barbed wire and defences. Obstacles were crushed under them as they created fear and confusion. In World War 1 they were a revolutionary addition to the battlefield and marked a significant shift in the way wars were fought.

Planes

At the start of World War 1 planes were still a relatively new invention. Military leaders soon recognized the potential of planes to gather information on enemy positions and movements. Initially they were used for observation but they soon evolved into combat roles. Early fighter planes were designed for air to air combat with machine guns mounted to shoot down enemy aircrafts. Later on they were loaded with bombs to drop on enemy targets. Those early days of aviation during World War 1 were thrilling eras of discovery and daring adventures. Pilots took to the air and became legends in their own way forever changing wars and inspiring future generations.

Submarines

Submarines were a game changer in World War 1, they could sneak up on enemy ships to make surprise attacks. They were able to dive beneath the ocean's soft surface and stealthily operate beneath the waves. The most famous submarines were the German U-boats. Submarines forced navies to adapt to their strategies. Anti-submarine warfare became a crucial aspect of naval operations with new technologies developed to detect and counter submarines. Ultimately submarines in World War 1 revolutionised naval warfare introducing stealth and surprise to seas.

Poison gas

Poison gas was one of the worst inventions of World War 1. Gas attacks were terrifying and deadly. Gases would drift across the battlefield unnoticed until it was too late. Soldiers exposed to poison gas experienced immense pain, finding it difficult to breathe and sustaining severe injuries. To protect themselves soldiers had to wear gas masks which made it uncomfortable and limited their effectiveness. Gas attacks caused fear and psychological trauma among many troops leading to many casualties and had long-lasting health problems for survivors. The use of poison gas during World War 1 was a dark chapter in the history of World War 1. After the war, the Geneva protocol of 1925 banned the use of chemical and biological weapons in warfare. Such devastating weapons that brought countless deaths and suffering to soldiers on both sides left a lasting legacy of horror. (Relations, 1972)

Communication

Effective communication was very important during World War 1 to ensure that troops coordinated orders and intelligence was gathered. Early on in the war carrier pigeons were used to fly long distances carrying important messages. Telegraph lines were set up on the frontlines to connect commanders with their headquarters and units. However these lines were often vulnerable to sabotage and disruption. Early radios and wireless communication were some of the other new communication technologies used during the war. They provided real-time communication between distant units. Messages were usually sent using morse code. This was a series of dots and dashes to transmit and decipher codes in secret. Overall all of these forms of communication during World War 1 were essential. Those who operated the systems played a vital role in ensuring that the messages reached the destinations accurately and swiftly.

Medical inventions and innovations

There were many medical inventions and innovations during World War I:

Triage Systems

Triage systems were used to determine who should receive treatment and care services based on their health status. Early triage systems were developed in World War 1 to categorise wounded soldiers based on their injuries and prioritising treatment accordingly. This was an important innovation that continues in modern emergency medical care.

Mobile Surgical Units

The establishment of mobile surgical units on the battlefields helped to quickly treat wounded soldiers. Later this evolved into modern field hospitals, which play a critical role in conflict zones and disaster relief efforts.

Blood Transfusions

Early medical advancements in World War 1 helped to develop innovations in blood transfusions to treat wounded soldiers. Ultimately this led to advancements in blood banking and storage techniques which have had a profound and lasting impact on modern medicine.

Gas Masks

The use of chemical weapons during World War 1 pushed the need to develop gas masks. These have since become a crucial piece of protection in both military and civilian settings.

X-ray

Early use of X-rays for diagnosing and locating bullets and shrapnel in wounded soldiers helped to advance medical diagnostics. This application of X-rays contributed significantly to the field of radiology.

Plastic Surgery

Innovations in plastic surgery played a crucial role in treating soldiers with disfiguring facial injuries. These advancements laid the foundation for modern reconstructive surgery.

Psychiatry

World War 1 highlighted the psychological toll of warfare, leading to increased research and treatment of various mental health issues. Such medical advancements from World War 1 not only improved the care and survival rates of wounded soldiers but also had a lasting effect on modern healthcare and medicine. (Office, 1925)

The impact of technology on World War 1

Technological advancements had a significant impact on World War 1. Overall they changed the nature of warfare with innovations that are used to this day. In the trenches stalemates were broken with the introduction of new weapons like machine guns and poison gas. Tanks helped to break through enemy lines. Planes added a new dimension to warfare enabling effective intelligence gathering, air combat and strategic bombing. Submarines disrupted naval operations and forced changes in tactics. Communications helped to gather and convey important information. Lastly, medical innovation was critical in healing wounded, brave soldiers.

Many of these innovations laid the foundation for future conflicts. The lessons learned from World War 1 led to the development of improved military and medical technology. After the war there were further advancements. Ultimately these innovations in the legacy of World War 1 were a pivotal moment in the evolution of modern warfare.

REFERENCES

PRIMARY REFERENCES

- This book is intended for informational and entertainment purposes only. Readers should not rely solely on its content for making important decisions or drawing conclusions. If you have concerns about the accuracy of any information presented in this book, please seek additional sources and expert advice.

- OpenAI. (2023). ChatGPT 3.5 https://chat.openai.com
This book was written with the assistance of ChatGPT, a language model developed by OpenAI, which provided creative input based on the information and instructions provided. While ChatGPT was used to aid in the writing process, the publishers of this book have made every effort to ensure the accuracy of the information presented. Extensive fact-checking and research were conducted to verify the information contained within this book.

- Mid Journey. (2023). https://www.midjourney.com/
All interior images were created with the use of artificial intelligence, namely Mid Journey.

- Wikipedia was a primary source of background details and structure.

    Wikipedia contributors. (2023, October 9). World War I - Wikipedia. https://en.wikipedia.org/wiki/World_War_I

OTHER REFERENCES

(Alphabetical order)

- Abbott, G. F. (2022). Greece and the Allies 1914-1922. DigiCat.
- Allenby, E. H. H. A. (2004). Allenby in Palestine: The Middle East Correspondence of Field Marshal Viscount Allenby, June 1917-October 1919.
- Brooks, J. (2016). The Battle of Jutland. Cambridge University Press.
- Bull, S. (2002). World War I Trench Warfare (1): 1914–16. Osprey Publishing.

- Butcher, T. (2014). The trigger: Hunting the Assassin Who Brought the World to War. Random House.
- Byers, A. (2017). The Treaty of Versailles and the League of Nations. Cavendish Square Publishing, LLC.
- Cave, N., & Sheldon, J. (2007). The Battle for Vimy Ridge, 1917. Casemate Publishers.
- Daley, P. (2009). Beersheba: A Journey Through Australia's Forgotten War. Melbourne Univ. Publishing.
- Darwin, C. (n.d.). On Evolution: The Development of the Theory of Natural Selection. Hackett Publishing.
- DiNardo, R. L. (2010). Breakthrough: The Gorlice-Tarnow Campaign, 1915. Bloomsbury Publishing USA.
- Dowling, T. (2008). The Brusilov offensive. Indiana University Press.
- Editors, C. R. (2017). The rise of Nazi Germany: The History of the Events That Brought Adolf Hitler to Power. Createspace Independent Publishing Platform.
- Editors, C. R. (2019). Osman I: The Life and Legacy of the Ottoman Empire's First Sultan. Independently Published.
- Fenby, J. (2014). The siege of Tsingtao: The only battle of the First World War to be fought in East Asia: how it came about and why its aftermath is still relevant today: Penguin Specials. Penguin Group Australia.
- Foley, R. (2012). Alfred von Schlieffen's military writings. Routledge.
- Gaudi, R. (2017). African Kaiser: General Paul Von Lettow-Vorbeck and the Great War in Africa. Oxford University Press.
- Grainger, J. D., & Grainger, T. O. H. J. D. (2006). The Battle for Palestine 1917. Boydell Press.
- Gray, E. A. (1994). The U-Boat War: 1914-1918. Pen and Sword.
- Grehan, J., & Mace, M. (2014). Western Front 1917-1918. Pen and Sword.
- Hall, R. C. (2010). Balkan Breakthrough: The Battle of Dobro Pole 1918. Indiana University Press.
- Hall, R. C. (2014). War in the Balkans: An Encyclopedic History from the Fall of the Ottoman Empire to the Breakup of Yugoslavia. Bloomsbury Publishing USA.
- Hamilton, J. (2004). Events Leading To World War I. ABDO.
- Herwig, H. H. (2009). The Marne, 1914: The Opening of World War I and the Battle That Changed the World. Random House.

- Jankowski, P. (2014). Verdun: The Longest Battle of the Great War. Oxford University Press.
- Jordan, D., & Neiberg, M. S. (2014). The Eastern Front 1914–1920: From Tannenberg to the Russo-Polish War. Amber Books Ltd.
- Kévorkian, R. (2011). The Armenian genocide: A Complete History. Bloomsbury Publishing.
- King, G., & Woolmans, S. (2013). The assassination of the Archduke: Sarajevo 1914 and the Murder that Changed the World. Pan Macmillan.
- Langley, A. (2009). The Hundred Days offensive: The Allies' Push to Win World War I. Capstone.
- Leach, N. (2016). Second battle of Ypres.
- Lyon, J. (2015). Serbia and the Balkan Front, 1914: The Outbreak of the Great War. Bloomsbury Publishing.
- Magnes, J. L. (1919). Russia and Germany at Brest-Litovsk: A Documentary History of the Peace Negotiations.
- Marcuzzi, S. (2020). Britain and Italy in the era of the Great War: Defending and Forging Empires. Cambridge University Press.
- McElvaine, R. S. (2010). The Great Depression: America 1929-1941. Crown.
- McLean, G. (2009). Penguin Book of New Zealanders at War. Penguin Random House New Zealand Limited.
- McMeekin, S. (2017). The Russian Revolution: A New History. Hachette UK.
- Miller, F. P., F, V. A., & John, M. (2009). Austria-Hungary. Alphascript Publishing.
- Murphy, D. (2015). Breaking point of the French army: The Nivelle Offensive of 1917. Casemate Publishers.
- O'Sullivan, P. (2014). The sinking of the Lusitania. Gill & Macmillan Ltd.
- Office, U. S. S. (1925). The Medical Dept. of the U.S. Army in the World War.
- Powers, A. a. A., & Martin, L. (1924). The Treaty of Versailles, the Treaty of St. Germainen-Laye and the Treaty of Trianon.
- Prior, R., & Wilson, T. (2016). The Somme. Yale University Press.
- Relations, U. S. C. S. C. O. F. (1972). The Geneva Protocol of 1925: Hearings, Ninety-second Congress, First Session, on Executive J, 91st Congress, 2d Session . . .

- Riasanovsky, A. V., & Watson, W. E. (1991). Readings in Russian History. Kendall Hunt Publishing Company.
- Roberts, J. (2005). Benito Mussolini. Twenty-First Century Books.
- Seymour, C. (1921). Woodrow Wilson and the World War: A Chronicle of Our Own Times.
- States, U. (1918). Selective Service Act [of May 18, 1917] as amended [Oct. 6, 1917 and May 16 and 20, 1918], 65th Congress.
- Storey, N. R., & Housego, M. (2010). Women in the First World War. Shire Publications.
- Torrey, G. E. (1998). Romania and World War I: A Collection of Studies. Histria Books.
- Tuchman, B. (2014). The Zimmermann Telegram. Penguin UK.
- Turfan, N. (2000). Rise of the young Turks: Politics, the Military and Ottoman Collapse. I.B. Tauris.
- Vatikiotis, P. (2017). Politics and the military in Jordan: A Study of the Arab Legion, 1921-1957. Routledge.
- Wiest, A. (2014). The Western Front 1917–1918: From Vimy Ridge to Amiens and the Armistice. Amber Books Ltd.

OTHER BOOKS BY HISTORY BROUGHT ALIVE

Available now in Ebook, Paperback, Hardcover, and Audiobook in all regions.

For Kids:

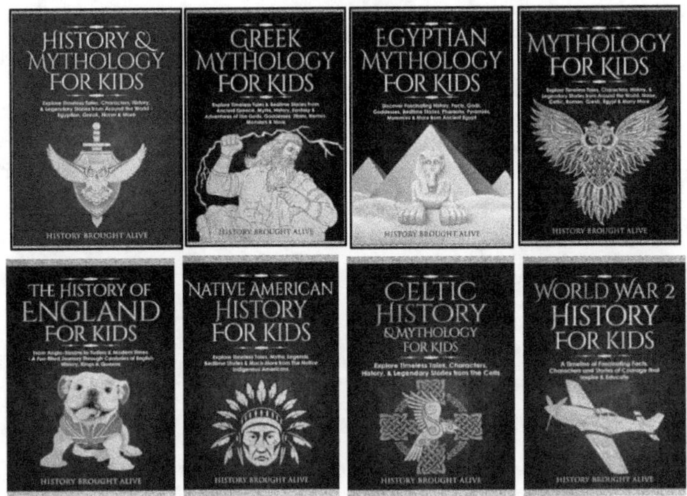

Other books:

www.ingramcontent.com/pod-product-compliance
Lightning Source LLC
Chambersburg PA
CBHW052031150726
48002CB00002B/548